LE

THE OL

LET'S READ
THE OLD TESTAMENT

RAYMOND BROWN

VICTORY PRESS
LONDON and EASTBOURNE

ISBN 0 85476 105 5

Scripture quotations are
from the Revised Standard
Version unless otherwise
stated.

Printed in Great Britain for
VICTORY PRESS (Evangelical Publishers Ltd)
Lottbridge Drove, Eastbourne, Sussex
by Richard Clay (The Chaucer Press) Ltd,
Bungay, Suffolk

CONTENTS

More than a Book   7

Here's the Beginning   9

Multitudes on the March   15

A Text Book for Priests   22

Ruin en route   28

The Word we Need   35

A Captain and His Invincible Commander   42

Doing What we Like   49

A Refugee's Reward   55

Give Us a King   60

Hollow Crowns   70

A Priest Looks at the Throne   83

Men with Difficult Tasks   91

Palace Steward becomes Successful Building
    Convener   97

God's Timing is Perfect   102

Even Suffering has its Value   105

The Finest Hymn Book in the World   110

This Way to Happiness   113

A Gloomy Man Speaks Out   117

True Love and its Tests   120

A Greater Miracle than the Exodus   124

The Call of a Sensitive Youth   130

A Sad Song with a Great Message   134

Preacher to the Prisoners   135

Heroism in Dark Days   139
A Marriage Breakdown and its Message   143
A Chance to Begin Again   148
The Shepherd who had to Preach   151
A Straight Word about Justice   156
The Prophet who Ran Away   158
Trouble on the Horizon   161
The End of a Cruel Nation   166
A View from the Tower   169
When God Shines His Lamp   172
Give God First Place   176
A View of the Beyond   180
Love Offers its Best   185
Old Testament Kings and Prophets   188

More than a Book

THE Bible is far more than a book; it is a library. The various books upon its shelves do not belong to any one type. In reading a biblical book many things have to be borne in mind. For one thing, historical background is important; the books in this library do not belong to one particular century. Some of the stories come from times when men lived in exceptionally primitive conditions; others reflect the thinking and living of a luxurious social background with highly advanced forms of civilisation. It is not only the date of each book which is important; the social, intellectual and cultural interests of each of the various authors and their contemporaries need some kind of simple introduction to a modern reading public. In the writing of the entire Bible, God used over forty writers from different backgrounds. The style of the various books is different as well. Many are history books, and alongside them you will find hymn books, books containing the messages given at different periods by the Hebrew prophets and books full of wise, practical sayings about everyday life. There are books which reflect on the glories of the past and others which make you think about the wonders of the future. There are later additions to this unique library which, in the New Testament, take the form of 'private papers', personal letters written to individuals in need, while others were addressed to groups of first-century Christians who were looking to some fine leader for a word to sustain them in difficult days.

The *Old Testament* forms the first main section of this library. Many people who want to understand the message of the whole Bible encounter difficulties when they start to read the Old Testament and, like the Ethiopian traveller about whom we read in the Acts of the Apostles (8 : 26–39), they wish there was somone to guide them in their study. This book has been written in the hope that it might at least go part of the way in meeting this kind of need. It is important to make it clear at the outset, however, that it will not help you very much if you merely read *this* book : it must be read alongside the various biblical books it seeks to explain. Because space is limited, it is not possible to pay special attention to difficult verses or passages which might well be interpreted in more than one way, but once the reader has covered an elementary course of study, then it becomes possible to give more careful attention to the various books of the Old Testament. The Scripture Union *Bible Study Books* can be warmly recommended in this connection, and help of a more detailed nature can be found in the *New Bible Commentary Revised* (Inter-Varsity Press).

This simple introduction to the Old Testament is written out of the deep conviction that the books of this library have an immense amount to say to the Christian today. The apostle Paul believed that all these books were profitable for believers (2 Tim. 3 : 16) and were written for our learning (Rom. 15 : 4) so, as we read them, we will look carefully at some of their important lessons about the Christian life. Let us pray with David, and say : 'Lord, open my eyes, that I may behold wondrous things out of Thy law'. (Psa. 119 : 18).

Here's the Beginning

THE first book in the library is called '*Genesis*'. The word simply means 'origin' or 'beginning'. It stands there to remind us that the Bible is about God and His dealings with men, not merely about men and their strivings after God. This distinction is important. It makes it plain that in spiritual things the initiative is with God. He made the world. He loved men. He longed that men would walk with Him in companionship, reliance and service, but this was spoilt by sin. The book of Genesis tells the story of the making of the world, the tragedy of man's sinful rebellion against God, and of how in various ways God came to man, pleading with him to repent and change. Genesis can be divided into two main sections:

1. THE WORLD AND ITS MAKER (Chapters 1–11)

The first two chapters present us with a magnificent portrait of the creation of the world. It must be remembered that this is a literary account of a marvellous achievement and not a detailed scientific survey. It is a portrait rather than a photograph. It is there at the very beginning of the Bible to assert a number of great facts and to outline a number of immense themes which would later be developed throughout the whole of the Bible in a variety of different forms. For one thing the creation story says *God's Word is powerful* ('And God said, "Let there be light"; and there was light', 1:3).

Whenever God issues an order, something happens. He
never speaks in vain (Isa. 55 : 11). The key phrase here is
'and it was so' (1 : 7, 9, 11, 15, 24, 30). How wonderful
that, right at the beginning of the Bible, we should be
reminded of the power of God's Word. If He wants to
achieve anything, He just says the word. The Bible is
God's Word and it will accomplish His purposes in our
lives. Read John 4:46–54 in this connection and note
that it was when Jesus spoke that powerful word 'Your
son will live' that the boy started to get better. The
Genesis creation stories also tell us that *God's work is
good*. 'God saw that it was good' is another recurrent
saying (1:4, 10, 12, 18, 21, 25, 31). It was a beautiful
world that God made. Sin defaced its magnificence
in many ways but it still shows us something of
God's greatness and glory (Psa. 8:3–9, 19:1–6, Rom.
1:19, 20). Further, *God's way is kind*. He knew that,
even though the world around was so magnificent and
that the man He had made could count upon His unfailing companionship (3:8), he still might be lonely.
So He made him a partner (2:18) and into this wonderful world came the priceless gift of human love.
Note, finally, that *God's will is best*. God came and
spoke a further word—to warn man and to instruct
him. A tree was set in that first garden which man was
forbidden to touch (2:16, 17). God said quite clearly
'You shall not eat'. All other fruits were for his enjoy-
ment, but this was not his to take. Possibly the very prohibition was meant to strengthen man's sense of reliance
on God. He was not to take of that tree to discern
whether something was right or wrong; he was meant to
listen to God's voice about such matters. We do not
always understand everything about the demands of
God upon our lives, but how much better to obey Him

than ignore Him.

The story of man's disobedience follows (3:1–24) and then these first pages of history tell their depressing tale—jealousy (4:5), murder (4:8), fear (4:14), immorality (6:4–6) and pride (11:4). The sad tale of Chapters 3–11 is only relieved by the heroism and devotion of a few like Abel (4:4, Heb. 11:4), Enoch (5:21–24, Heb. 11:5) and Noah (6:8, Heb. 11:7). For the rest, there is a recurring phrase which underlines the story of man's sin: 'and he died' (5:5, 8, 11, 14, 17, 20, 27, 31). This is just what God had said would happen if man disobeyed him (2:17). Notice too how quickly sin spreads from an individual (3:1) to a couple (3:12), then to a family (4:1–15) and finally to the whole world (11:1–9).

2. THE FAITH AND ITS HEROES (Chapters 12–50)

In the remaining chapters of this important book we are introduced to four great personalities. We are here able to see not only how God deals with individuals but how, through their changed lives, He brings help to others.

(i) *Abraham: the man God called* (Chapters 12–23)

To Adam God had given a necessary word of warning ('You shall not . . .'); to Abraham (at first called Abram) he issued an exciting command about an adventurous opportunity, 'Go from your country' (12:1). God was to make this unique figure the founder of the most important community in the world, Israel, the people of God. Adam replied in disobedience (Rom. 5:12), but Abraham responded in immediate obedience and dependent faith. He stepped out on that long, unknown journey (12:4, 5) and proved that those who obey

God's voice enjoy God's presence (12:7). Not that the story of Abraham is a completely unspoilt account of godliness and trust. He too made his mistakes (e.g. 12:10-20, 20:1-18) but he was worshipful (12:8), unselfish (13:8-11), courageous (14:1-16), trusting (15:6), compassionate (17:18), hospitable (18:1-5) and prayerful (18:16-33). The story of Abraham begins with a call to obedience and ends on the same theme but with an even more difficult command. In the first chapter of his story (12) God asks him to leave his relations (12:1) but in the final test he is asked to offer his only son as a sacrifice (22). It seemed such a strange and even heartless request to make. But Abraham believed God and knew that, if He had asked him to do something, it must be to some good purpose. The experience tested the reality of his faith, showed his genuine love for God, and provided us all with a portrait of an even greater Offering. It foreshadowed a day when our heavenly Father gave His only Son. Chapter 23 records the death of Sarah and Abraham's provision of a burying place for his wife and family.

(ii) *Isaac: the man God led* (Chapters 24-26)

The son who was spared (22:12, 13) followed in the steps of his godly father. There is not as much about him in the book, but a few chapters tell of how God provided a partner for him (24:1-67), made him a father in answer to earnest prayer (25:20, 21), gave him food in a time of famine (26:1-14) and helped him to make provision for the future by prompting him to open some disused and neglected wells (26:18-22). 'Altar', 'tent' and 'well' all appear in one verse (26:25) in the Isaac story. They symbolise his attitude to life. Isaac believed it important for a man to discern his priorities (the altar), remember his pilgrimage (the tent, cf. Heb. 11:8–10) and use his resources (the wells).

(iii) *Jacob: the man God changed* (Chapters 27–36)

Isaac's wife, Rebekah, gave birth to twins (25:21–26). The boys were very different in personality, outlook and interests. Esau lived for the present (25:29–34) while Jacob had a keen eye to the future. Jacob's cunning schemes created a division between the brothers and the ensuing story is not a happy one (27:1–46). Jacob was hardly a pleasant man to know, but he illustrates the generous love and kindness of God who does not bless us because we deserve it but because we need it. God met with him (28:11–22) and provided him with a wife (29:1–30) and children (30:1–26). Jacob had various family difficulties (31:1–55) and many of the tragedies that followed were due to his own lack of wisdom and love. But God robbed him of his self-reliance, transformed his character and changed his name (32:24–32). After a dramatic encounter with a messenger from God he was a different man.

(iv) *Joseph: the man God used* (Chapters 37–50)

Jacob's favourite son was named Joseph. The remaining chapters of Genesis tell the story of his life and work. Despised by his brothers, he was sold to a group of passing tradesmen for slavery in Egypt (37:1–35). He was later employed in a prosperous Egyptian home but his purity of mind and strength of will soon cost him his freedom. During a period of unjust imprisonment he made some kind of reputation as an interpreter of dreams. All the near-eastern people believed that dreams had unique significance and Joseph's interpretation of the dream of Egypt's ruler ultimately led to his appointment as the senior state official (40:1–41:57). A serious famine caused his brothers to come to Egypt looking for food and this eventually led to a family re-union (42:1–46:34). Joseph was able to care for his father and brothers throughout a difficult period (47:1–28).

In his extreme old age Jacob pronounced a blessing on Joseph and his two sons (48:1–22) as well as on his own sons (49:1–33). Joseph's brothers feared for their lives once Jacob had died. They imagined that their influential brother would punish them for their cruelty to him many years before (50:15). How little they knew him. Nobody could deny that he had suffered at their hands. His own father had recognised this at the end of his days (49:22–24), but Joseph had unlimited spiritual resources. Like his grandfather, Isaac, he knew how to dig a well (49:22). Isaac's wells were scattered throughout the land but Joseph had secret springs of peace and patience. They satisfied his thirst through many a difficult day, even when life was like a battle-field (49:23, 24). Thinking back on his brothers' bitterness and the trials that followed, he made a magnificent confession of faith and confidence. Turning to his now repentant brothers he said: 'As for you, you meant evil against me, but God meant it for good' (50:20). Joseph knew that God had used this tragedy for His own purposes. The day they threw him down that pit in Dothan (37:24) they began a series of divinely ordained events destined to make their unwanted brother into a leader and counsellor whose skill and insight would bring hope to thousands. God has a plan for all our lives.

Multitudes on the March

AT the end of the *Book of Genesis*, God's people were enjoying life in Egypt. Their famine days were over and the comfort and security of a new land had brought immense enrichment to them all. Their acceptance by the Egyptians was due to the indebtedness of the nationals to Joseph. He had given them such strong and wise leadership that the least they could do was to provide shelter for his large family. *Exodus* follows Genesis continuing the story of God's people but it opens in a later era : 'There arose a new king over Egypt, who did not know Joseph' (1 : 8). By this time the Israelites had multiplied; vast numbers of Hebrew people were to be seen in many parts of the land. The new king ordered that all these foreigners be assigned to rigorous slave duties (1. 9–14) and, in order to reduce their numbers, every boy born into an Israelite home had to be slain at birth (1 : 15–22). The opening chapters set the scene for the story of God's deliverance. They tell how He raised up the right man for the necessary task. In the closing chapters of Genesis, we are told how He raised up Joseph for a special mission. Now in the opening chapters of the next book we see how He chose Moses for another task. God always has a man or woman suitable for His work, but they are not always willing to serve. Joseph was an eager and willing worker, but Moses was reluctant to begin his difficult assignment. Let us turn now to the plan and design of this book in which the story is told. It can be divided into two main parts: God's man (1–18) and God's message (19–40).

1. GOD'S MAN (Chapters 1–18)

The enslaved people (1:1–22) needed someone who would lead them out of Egyptian captivity and take them to the land God had originally promised to them (Gen. 12:1–3; 13:14–18). God had such a man in mind. His name was Moses. When he was born he was hidden in his home for three months, but after that time it was impossible to keep his birth a secret. The family devised a plan to keep him alive and, under the merciful protection of God, this little boy was given an honoured place in the wealthiest home in Egypt (2:1–10). As he grew up Moses became aware of his people's slavery and grief. One day he slew an Egyptian task-master who was being cruel to a Hebrew slave and the news got back to the king's household (2:11–15). The life of Moses was now in serious danger and he fled from the country to the land of Midian, where he was received into the family of a local priest (2:16–25). Moses' life was dramatically changed from that of a courtier to a shepherd, but God was guiding his steps and both stages of his life were of immense importance.

In the providence of God little is wasted. There is a divine economy at work in the ordering of our lives, even when we are not aware of it. The education and upbringing Moses received at an Egytian court provided him with rich intellectual resources; all this would be needed for the task God had in mind for him. His long period of service as a shepherd stood him in great stead as a pastor of God's people. Those years of quiet reflection gave him a spiritual depth which it might have been difficult to have acquired in all the worldly activity

of a pagan palace. Once he was ready for his divinely
ordained task, God spoke to Moses about the plan of
deliverance (3:1-10). But Moses was terrified at the
prospect and one excuse tumbled out after another. He
was sure that there were far more suitable men for such
a highly important mission (3:11-4:17)! Eventually,
though reluctantly, he went to the royal palace in
obedience to God (4:18-31). Naturally, the king of
Egypt was quite unwilling to release all his slaves. They
had worked well and he needed them for further building projects. The refusal to release them was followed
by a series of plagues designed to bring the Egyptians to
the place of entire submission to God's will in this
matter. The plagues increased in seriousness and brought
havoc throughout the land but the king still refused to
let the Israelites go free (5:1-11, 10).

The most serious plague was left until last. Throughout the years the Egyptians had brought distress to
thousands of Hebrew parents by the killing of every
baby boy that was born in their homes. Now the wrath
of God would come upon them and the eldest child in
every Egyptian home would die on an appointed night.
The details of the story record the institution of the
Passover (12:1-29), a commemorative feast kept by
the Hebrew people throughout the centuries to remind
them of this act of deliverance. In the course of the
Passover an unblemished lamb was offered as a sacrifice
and its blood sprinkled around the doorpost of every
Hebrew home. On that dreadful night the threatened
judgment came. The Lord's angel passed over every
home where the blood could be seen and all who sheltered in that place were saved. It is a striking picture of
a greater deliverance later to be accomplished by Christ,
our Paschal Lamb. (1 Cor. 5:7, cf. John 1:29; 19:36;

B

1 Pet. 1 : 19). The obedience of the Hebrew slaves made
their deliverance possible. God told them what they had
to do and they acted upon it. In Chapter 12, therefore,
the theme is *obey Him*. We too can be delivered from
the bondage of our sins, but obedience to God's Word is
a necessary condition (cf. Heb. 5 : 9; 1 Pet. 4 : 17).

In the following chapters the developing story continues to illustrate our relationship with God. We must
serve Him (13 : 1–16). The firstborn of every Egyptian
household had just been slain; therefore, as an act of
gratitude, the firstborn in every Hebrew family must
be presented to the Lord. These spared lives must be
given over to God for service and witness. We too are
saved in order to serve. Our salvation is not designed
solely for our security but for God's glory and the blessing of others. Further, we must *trust Him* (14 : 1–31).
The Egyptians soon recovered from their shock and pursued the Hebrew slaves. They had lost so many able
bodied people through the judgment of God that the
slaves could not possibly be spared. The Israelites looked
back and saw the huge contingents of Egyptian soldiers,
angry and eager for vengeance. But the terrified slaves
heard their leader as he spoke a strengthening word
from God Himself : 'Fear not, stand firm, and see the
salvation of the Lord, which He will work for you today
. . . The Lord will fight for you, and you have only to be
still' (14 : 13, 14). The command to 'stand still' was
clearly a warning against the dangers of panic. Hundreds of frightened people might rush in all directions
and hurt their fellow-travellers. It was vital at this time
to believe that God could and would deliver them. The
mighty act of deliverance came, and the next two chapters (15 : 1–16 : 36) remind us that we should *thank
Him*. The 'song of Moses' is a triumphant hymn of

praise for the mercies of that great day (15 : 1–27)
while Chapter 16 records a further theme for thanksgiving—God's provision for the needs of every day.

Once the problems of thirst (15 : 22–27; 17 : 1–7)
and hunger (16 : 1–36) had been miraculously overcome
they met further trouble; a troop of Amalekite soldiers
came to intercept the Israelite travellers. Moses knew
that this emergency situation, as all others, called for
prayer. He ascended a nearby mountain and lifted up
his hands in believing prayer. There is a further lesson
here for us. In our troubles, we must *seek Him* (17 : 8–
16).

The concluding chapter of this first main section of
Exodus has something to say about the importance of
team-work in God's service. Jethro, the father-in-law of
Moses, knew that the people's gifted leader could not
carry all these responsibilities on his own shoulders. He
needed a group of trustworthy helpers (18 : 1–27) who
would look after the legal and domestic affairs of smaller
companies. Only the more serious problems would be
referred to Moses himself. Once Jethro had given this
excellent advice, he returned to his own country. His
words about designating work and sharing responsibilities were to play no mean part in the later revelation
which God gave to Moses about the various duties in
God's service which had to be shared by a vast number
of willing people.

2. GOD'S MESSAGE (Chapters 19–40)

The second main section in this book deals with the
giving of the Law to Moses. These people had a long
journey ahead and they needed clear guidance and firm
rules for the days before them. The Ten Commandments
form the basis; this was their code of conduct for the

future (20 : 1–17). The first five commandments emphasise their walk with God, while the remaining five
outline their responsibility towards men. The following chapters develop these ideas and particularise some
of the basic legislation. They stress the importance of
love, honesty and justice—vital elements in the administration of any well-ordered community (20 : 18–
24 : 18).

Moses then heard a further word from God, not now
concerning behaviour among men but about man's approach to the Lord God. The next group of chapters give
instruction about the tabernacle, the portable 'temple',
designed to provide a central place of worship in the
camp and to focus the daily attention of this vast company of pilgrims on the realities of the spiritual life.
The tabernacle's intricate and meaningful design is given
in detail together with regulations concerning those who
should officiate in this special place of worship (priests)
and the offerings they should present (25 : 1–31 : 18).
After hearing these laws about pure worship, imagine
the horror of Moses when he descended the mountain
and saw that the people were offering their adoration to
forbidden idols (32 : 1–35). The people soon realised
their mistake, but it was one further indication of their
inbred disobedience and stubborn rebellion. God's word
to them had been unmistakably clear : 'Obey my voice
and keep my covenant' (19 : 5) and they had obviously
disappointed Him. But, in generous mercy, God forgave
them, and their offerings for the tabernacle were accepted (33 : 1–35 : 29).

Jethro had said something to his son-in-law about the
distribution of work, and those principles now came
into operation in a remarkable way. Gifts were brought
and numerous craftsmen offered their different skills in

the making of this magnificent tabernacle (35:30–40:38). Their place of worship was to be given a daily sign of God's abiding presence. When the 'cloud of the Lord' was resting, they knew that they must stay in that particular area. As it moved they were to strike camp and steadily follow that symbol of God's nearness. In this way, worship was related to life. God's presence among them assured every pilgrim of His constant protection and unfailing guidance.

We too have a 'Tabernacle'. It is no longer a place; it is a Person. When the Lord Jesus came into the world it was said of Him that He 'dwelt among us'. The word there in John 1. 14 means 'pitched his tent'; He tabernacled among men. He is our means of access to God. He assures us all of God's unchanging presence and points to the only route for a happy and useful life as He says 'I am the Way' (John 14:6).

Before the tabernacle was constructed the doubters among the Israelite pilgrims could say 'Is the Lord among us or not?' (17:7). Now they had been given a visible symbol of His presence in their camp. Later generations were to think of Christ and say 'Behold the tabernacle of God is with men' (Rev. 21:3, AV).

A Text Book for Priests

THE third book in this collection which is clearly associated with the name of Moses is called *Leviticus*. Like the two earlier books in the collection its title is derived from that given to it in the Greek version of the Old Testament (called the *Septuagint*, because it was reputed to be the work of *seventy* translators). Many of its rules and regulations seem strange to us but we have to remember that these laws were for the necessary guidance of God's people in their spiritual infancy. Just as we try to convey truth to children with the aid of pictures and models, so the Lord graciously taught His own people with the help of some visual aids. The book can be divided into three parts. The first seven chapters deal with some aspects of their sacrificial system. Then a short section pays attention to the priesthood, while the remaining chapters outline a series of instructions affecting the welfare of the pilgrim people and provide details regarding their religious festivals.

1. SACRIFICES (Chapters 1–7)

A series of offerings are outlined in the opening chapters (1–7). These include *the burnt offering* which was offered to God in its entirety (1:1–17). With most offerings a portion was retained for the priest and also for the offerer. As he ate part of the offering, it symbolised his communion with the God he loved and adored. But with the burnt offering it was offered completely to the Lord. It was *extremely costly* ('a male without blemish', 1 : 3)—only the best could be given. It was *entirely voluntary* (1 : 3, AV); there must be no element of compulsion about it other than the inner compulsion of gratitude and worship. It was *unashamedly public*. It had to be offered 'at the door of the tent of meeting' (1 : 3). We too have an offering to make which is costly, voluntary and must become evident to all. It is the total submission of our bodies for God's service (Rom. 12 : 1, 2).

After the burnt offering, there is detailed instruction about a *cereal offering*, also a voluntary sacrifice (2 : 1–16), a large portion of which was given to the priests; a *peace offering* (3 : 1–17) only part of which was burnt and the rest shared by the offerer among his family and friends; a *sin offering* (4 : 1–5 : 13) made for sins of ignorance (note that for sins of absolute rebellion and defiance 'with a high hand' (Num. 15 : 30) there was no sacrifice available) and a *guilt offering* (5 : 14–6 : 7) which was primarily for trespasses which demanded some form of restitution. If things had to be put right, then all that must be done before the guilt offering was presented. Further instruction is given about the portion of these offerings which had to be handed to the priest and that which should be shared by the offerer among his family and friends (6 : 8–7 : 38).

2. PRIESTS (Chapters 8–10)

For this elaborate sacrificial worship, properly appointed servants were necessary and the next three chapters describe the men God had in mind for these sacred duties. Note that these men were *chosen*. It was not the kind of work that anyone could do. The responsibilities fall on a select group ('Aaron and his sons',

8:1). They also had to be *cleansed* (8:6) and then *clothed* with special garments (8:7–9). After an appropriate sacrifice had been offered (8:10–22) the shed blood was used to anoint these men for service. Moses put this sacrificial blood on the right ear, thumb and big toe of each man who had been set aside for these holy tasks.

Now that Christ has come as our great High Priest (Heb. 1:3; 5:1–10; 7:25) we no longer need priestly intermediaries. All of us share in a priestly ministry if we are true believers. But serving as a priest is a costly business. It is significant that the two New Testament books where Christians are described as priests (1 Pet. 2:5, 9; Rev. 1:6) were written to believers who had encountered fierce persecution. It is not easy to be a believer-priest. Like the priests in these chapters of Leviticus we too are *chosen* (John 15:16), *cleansed* (1 John 1:9) and must be *clothed* in garments of righteous living (Rom. 13:12–14; Rev. 7:14). We too have sacrifices to offer (Rom. 12:1, 2; Heb. 13:15, 16; 1 Pet. 2:5). They are not blood sacrifices but they are costly.

The two chapters which follow the story of the anointing of the Levitical priests (9:1–10:11) present us with two sharply contrasting pictures. Chapter 9 describes the utter obedience of Aaron and his priestly associates but Chapter 10 narrates a sad tale of disobedience, rivalry and presumption. Nadab and Abihu did peculiar things with some kind of fire offering 'and offered unholy fire before the Lord, such as he had not commanded them' (10:1). Only the high priest was permitted to offer incense (Exod. 30:7–9). Their presumptuous act may have been prompted by some form of jealousy and rivalry. It was a warning to those priests of that time that they must not only *do* what God had commanded; they must also *refrain from doing* what he had not commanded.

3. RULES (Chapters 11–27)

The third section of this book deals with a series of rules which were of importance in the spiritual life of the community.

The regulations deal first of all with various aspects of *ceremonial purity* (11–15). In these five chapters the fear of the unclean is a most important issue. The word 'unclean' (defiled) is found over a hundred times in these few chapters. Certain animals were regarded as unsuitable for eating, so were various sea creatures, birds and insects (11:1–47). Simple purificatory rites were demanded after childbirth (12:1–8), rules are given concerning leprosy (13:1–14:57) and physical discharges of various kinds (15:1–33). These detailed prohibitions and requirements seem strange to us, but they emphasise the purity-theme, a most important one in *Leviticus* where a key-idea is that of 'holiness' (11:44, 45; 19:2; 20:7, 26; 1 Pet. 1:16).

The idea of *inward purity* emerges at this point in the book and the legislation is given regarding the famous Day of Atonement (16:1–34, cf. 23:27 f.; 25:9). It is recognised that man needs to be inwardly as well as outwardly clean. The provisions of the Day of Atonement were designed to bring the assurance of forgiveness to the entire Israelite community. A bullock and a ram were sacrificed, then two goats were introduced into the ceremony. Confession of sin was made on behalf of the whole assembly by the high-priest as he laid his hands on the head of the goat chosen for sacrifice. The remaining live goat (a scapegoat) was later released and sent into the wilderness. It was a vivid picture of the carrying away of the sins of the people. The thought may even have been in the mind of John the Baptist as he described Jesus as the One 'who takes away the sin of the world' (John 1 : 29). We know that our sins are forgiven because Jesus has 'carried' (1 Pet. 2 : 24 margin) our sins up to His Cross. Further detail about sacrifice is found in the next chapter (17 : 1–16). This passage emphasises the importance of the blood in the sacrificial offerings (17 : 11). The Bible clearly declares the truth that 'without the shedding of blood there is no forgiveness of sins' (Heb. 9 : 22) and the Lord Jesus knew that His outpoured blood would effect man's forgiveness, reconciliation with God, peace and liberty (Matt. 26 : 28; Mark 14 : 24; Rom. 3 : 25; 5 : 9; Eph. 1 : 7; 2 : 13; Col. 1 : 14, 20; Heb. 12 : 24; 13 : 20; Rev. 1 : 5).

The third group of rules in this section focus on the importance of *moral purity* (18 : 1–20 : 27). A high moral standard was vital. In the interests of community welfare certain prohibitions were made abundantly clear. The declining moral standards of our own day will inevitably lead to widespread heart-ache and universal sadness. Whenever men ignore God's laws they bring grief upon themselves. In a moral universe men can only be happy as they obey Him. This is how God has designed it. If we insist on ignoring the commands of God, we will do so to our own hurt as well as to our ultimate shame.

Several of these chapters are concerned specifically with priestly legislation but they frequently remind the whole company of the need for holiness. (19 : 2, cf. 1 Pet. 1 : 16; 2 : 5). Purity of life is not only demanded of those who are called to specific forms of service; all God's people must be holy. They must also be *generous*

(19:9–10), *honest* (19:11–13) and *kind* (19:14–18), as well as *pure* (19:19–22). Various instructions are given regarding serious community offences (19:23–20:27) after which the regulations regarding various aspects of priesthood are listed. These include the particular need of holiness throughout the priesthood (21:1–9), the requirements of the high-priest (21:10–15) and the physical deformities and defilements which prevent any man from serving as a priest (21:16–22:16). Instruction is then given to the priests about sacrificial offerings (22:17–33), the weekly and annual festivals (23:1–44), the oil and bread used in the Tabernacle (24:1–9) and the sins of cursing and cruelty (24:10–23). Rules follow regarding the Sabbatical and Jubilee years and the care of strangers (25:1–55). A series of blessings and cursings (26:1–46) and a passage about vows and tithes (27:1–34) brings this book to a close.

It is included in the Bible because we need to be reminded to put God first (1:1–17), rely on Him for pardon (16:1–34), keep clean (19:2) and love our fellows (19:10). We no longer need many of these visual aids but the great truths they enshrine will always be important.

Ruin en route

THE next book in the Bible's library has been given the unusual title of *Numbers*. The title says very little about the actual contents of the book itself and doubtless originates in the simple fact that several passages in the book are given over to numerical lists of one kind and another. The Hebrews originally called the book 'in the wilderness' (1 : 1) and that is a far more descriptive title for the story told in these pages. *Numbers* records a pathetic tale. It carries various details about the itinerary of the children of Israel, describes their wilderness wanderings, records their idolatry and immorality at all too frequent intervals and tells us about God's judgment upon them for their sins.

That all sounds very depressing, but we must remember that it is not *mere* history. There are a number of profound lessons in the book for ourselves. This, like all other biblical books, has been 'written for our instruction' (Rom. 15 : 4). Therefore, as we read this story of the Hebrew people and their travels, we must think about ourselves and our walk with God. In the light of this book, we ought to ask whether we are in step with Him. We can only be really happy if we tread the path that is pleasing to Him. In the Bible, life is often portrayed as a journey. The Word of God recognises that it is easy to take a turn in the wrong direction and this is what *Numbers* is all about. The children of Israel made a number of grave mistakes and they are openly recorded in this story. As we survey the book, let us think about God's dealings with His people:

1. GOD TEACHES HIS PEOPLE (Chapters 1–8)

The opening chapters provide us with information about the composition and numerical strength of the various tribes. We are told that distinct places were assigned to them while they were in the camp and also as they were on the march. (1:1–2:34). Everything had to be done in an orderly way. The Lord knew that His people would never make that journey if they did not pay attention to practical details about the lay-out of the encampment and the order of tribes in the column of pilgrims as they marched. God loves order and design. He works according to a plan and expects his children to do things in a methodical way. The Levites were set aside as the servants of the priests and their responsibilities are described in this section (3:1–4:49). They had clearly defined responsibilities to help the priesthood in the administration of the community's *spiritual* life. But God is not only interested in spiritual matters; He also made provision for His people's *physical* well-being. Contact with certain diseases and physical abnormalities exposed the camp to obvious dangers, so clearly defined rules were recorded (5:1–10). The people's *moral* welfare was also His concern and this is discussed as well (5:11–31). Family life was extremely important and legislation was given to cover possible domestic upheavals.

Turning to brighter themes, people who, at some particular time of their life, had special cause for thanksgiving, could take a vow called 'The vow of a Nazarite'. It was a way of showing their indebtedness to God (6:1–21). The regulations demanded that anyone taking the vow must not eat or drink anything which came from the vine, they must not shave or cut their hair, neither must they come into contact with a dead body. They were to be regarded during the period of the vow as 'separated' or 'consecrated' to the Lord. The *vine* was an outward indication of the settled life. Pilgrims do not plant vines; it takes several years to establish a vineyard. Those who took this vow refrained from wine and the fruit of the vineyard in order to emphasise the *pilgrim* nature of a godly life. This world is not our home (1 Pet. 1 : 17; 2 : 11). Possibly the prohibition about cutting their hair may have been a way of publicly indicating that they had taken the vow. It could have been an act of *witness*; their dedication to God became obvious to the whole community. Believers certainly need to be reminded of this aspect of their consecration to the Lord. Further, death was regarded as having a defiling effect on the living. The dead body was a sign of the corruption that is due to man's sin. Nobody who took the Nazarite's vow was allowed to touch a dead body, either of a human being or of an animal. This is probably meant to stress the *holiness* theme again. So, in the Nazarite vow we have a portrait of the dedicated life, of pilgrimage, witness and holiness.

Appropriately enough, the details about this unusual vow (what men can do for God) is followed by some memorable words about what God will do for men (6 : 22–27). This priestly benediction has brought peace and strength to God's people throughout the centuries. It has reminded believers in every generation of His keeping power, generous favour and abiding peace. The next two chapters (7 : 1–8 : 26) record the gifts brought by the various tribal leaders for the work of God and explain the way that the Levites were separated for their holy service. These two chapters form an interesting little study. They illustrate the fact that the work of God does not only require our offerings it also demands our complete dedication to the Lord who longs to use us as *people*. Money is not enough.

2. GOD GUIDES HIS PEOPLE (Chapters 9–10)

Chapter 9 tells us about the Passover festival as it was observed by God's people in the wilderness. Nobody could share in this great feast if they were unclean (e.g. defiled through touching a corpse) so they had to ask Moses for advice about this problem. God showed Moses what these people could do in these circumstances (9 : 1–14). The Passover reminded them all of how wonderfully God had guided them *in the past*. He had led them out of Egypt and set them on the road to freedom. But all that was behind them. What about their need for guidance in the present? He had provided the special cloud as a daily sign of His presence (9 : 15–23). That was God's way of guiding them and protecting them. Hostile tribes would be afraid of attacking them at night when they saw that great column of fire, and as it shed its light all over the camp of Israel nobody in those tents could possibly be afraid. When the cloud moved on then, *and only then*, were the Hebrew people to move. In order to rally the people at such a time two silver trumpets were made so that Moses could call the people to order (10 : 1–10). Certain sounds on the trumpet indicated different things. God thought of everything. He considers every detail in the planning of our lives too. Nothing escapes His notice. We also read of the part played by Hobab, a highly skilled Midianite guide (10 : 29–32). In addition to the cloud of His presence, God graciously provided the comfort of this human help.

3. GOD CORRECTS HIS PEOPLE (Chapters 11–20)

These passages relate a series of very sad events. First of all, the children of Israel remembered the past, and grumbled (11:1–6). They talked about the food they used to have when they were in Egypt—fish, cucumbers, melons, leeks, onions and garlic. Some of the crowd wished they had stayed by their lavish meal-tables way back in Egypt. Then, they thought about their present food, the manna, and grumbled (11:4–9). God was grieved about their ingratitude. Because they complained about their diet, He gave them extra food, some birds called quails, and the people ate them until they became seriously ill (11:10–35). The following chapters tell of divisions and quarrels, (12:1–16) unbelief and fear (13:1–33), rebellion and strife (14:1–10). Moses prayed for his disgruntled congregation (14:11–19) and the Lord graciously pardoned the sins of the people, but all those who persisted in their unbelief were told that they would never enter the Promised Land (14:20–45). Chapter 15 records some further laws, and we then read about yet another scene of discord and rebellion, followed by the inevitable judgment of God upon the rebels (16:1–50). A miraculous event is then narrated, the story of Aaron's blossoming rod. This miracle happened in order to prove to the people that the Levites were the divinely appointed tribe for privileged service (17:1–13), and the following chapters (18:1–19:22) record another series of regulations about special acts of worship and everyday life. Then, the grumbling begins again! This time the travellers are short of water and the people remembered all the delicious fruits they had in Egypt (20:1–5). Water was given to them by God (20:6–13), though in the course of this miraculous intervention Moses appears to have grieved God, perhaps by his unbelief or impatience (20:11-12). The king of Edom refused to let the pilgrims go through his territory (20:14-21), and at this difficult and frustrating part of the journey, Aaron died (20:22-29).

4. GOD HELPS HIS PEOPLE (Chapters 21-36)

This final section of *Numbers* illustrates how wonderfully God comes to His people's aid when they need Him. He fights their battles (21:1-35), and frustrates their enemies (22:1-24:25). God will also deliver us in our difficulties, if only we will trust Him. But the people did not always trust the Lord; sometimes they indulged in idolatry and immorality—the two often go together (25:1-18). The next chapter gives details of another census (26:1-65). Various matters are then discussed— the allocation of land to certain women in danger of losing their inheritance (27:1-11), the appointment of Joshua as the successor of Moses (27:12-23), and rules regarding certain offerings and vows (28:1-30:16). Details are then given regarding another conflict with the enemy, this time the Midianites (31:1-54). Once again the Lord helps His people. The final chapters provide us with information about the allocation of certain land to particular tribes, about the route of God's people thus far, and about cities of refuge and their purpose (32:1-35:34). A final passage reverts to the earlier question of land in respect of the women whose inheritance was in jeopardy (36:1-13).

Numbers is a bewildering book in some ways. Its style and arrangement is baffling. Lists of tribes are followed by accounts of historical events, regulations about sacrifice are given alongside details of intricate legal controversies. It is all very important as history for we want to

C

know the route of God's people as they made their way to the Promised Land, but what are the main lessons of this book for a Christian today? It reminds us that God is concerned about the practical details of everyday life. Some Christians think He is only interested in religion! His people's physical health was as important to God as their spiritual communion. Further, the book teaches us that God uses all sorts of people with their various gifts for His purposes. While it is true that specially appointed people had clearly defined responsibilites, everyone had work to do. The tabernacle worship depended as much on expert furniture removers as upon the priests who ministered there. In God's service there is work for everyone. It tells us also that when our gracious God makes a promise, He always keeps it (23 : 19). Further, the book reminds us of the seriousness of sin, and particularly of the impossibility of our hiding our sins from God (32 : 23). Finally, *Numbers* illustrates the fact that those who have 'wholly followed the Lord' (14 : 24, 32 : 12) bring delight to His heart and immense joy to their own.

The Word we Need

THE next book, *Deuteronomy*, completes the special set of five works often grouped together under the name of Moses and called 'The Pentateuch'. *Deuteronomy* simply means 'second law'. This is derived from a Greek translation of one particular phrase in the book (17:18). It is not a very helpful title as it suggests that the book is only a repetition of earlier teaching. Although some material is repeated, Deuteronomy contains something quite new, and we must begin by noting what it is. Throughout the Near East whenever two kings wanted to make some kind of covenant or agreement, a special kind of treaty was drawn up. These treaties followed clearly defined patterns, and their design was something like this: they began with a statement about the author of the treaty, then some historical detail was provided followed by the stipulations and requirements. The treaty was concluded by giving details of the succession arrangements (should the author die) and a final passage mentioned a series of blessings (should the treaty be kept) and cursings (should it be broken).

Even a glance at *Deuteronomy* shows that the book roughly follows this treaty-plan. In other words, this is the treaty which the Lord God makes with His people. It is not a treaty between equals. He is the supreme God, but He loves men and declares Himself to them (1:6). Historical detail is given as in a secular treaty (1:1–

4:49) and stipulations follow (5:1–26:19) after which an extended passage lists certain blessings and cursings (27:1–30:20). The final section of *Deuteronomy* deals with succession arrangements as Moses hands over to Joshua (31:1–34:12). The arrangement of teaching in the book suggests that it may well have been influenced by the treaty-pattern.

For our purposes the book can be divided quite simply into three unequal parts:

1. GOD'S ACTS (Chapters 1–4)

It has been said that God is known for what He is by what He does. History is something more than the gradual unfolding of chance events. Throughout the Bible we see that God's children were aware of His guiding Hand in their personal, national and even international affairs. Therefore, *Deuteronomy* begins by telling us about the mighty acts of God. Sadly, it also has to relate something of the disobedience and transgression of men (1:26–46). This first section lays an important historical foundation for the later message of the book.

2. GOD'S LAWS (Chapters 5–30)

This main section contains a series of laws, exhortations and injunctions about various aspects of life. The passage found at the beginning (5:1–27) reminds the gathered congregation of the Ten Commandments given at Horeb and they are told that these must not be left way back in antiquity but carefully passed on to their children throughout the succeeding generations (5:28–6:25). Moreover, these laws are not only to be taught, but obeyed (7:1–11:32). If the people do not obey, they will soon be given over to idolatry instead of pure wor-

ship (12 : 1–16 : 22). A man's life cannot endure a
spiritual vacuum. If love for God goes out, then something evil will replace it. It becomes obvious as one reads
the following chapters that, as we have seen in our previous studies, a man's spirituality is closely related to
everything that he does in life—legal matters, domestic
regulations, community behaviour are discussed as
issues that are of the greatest possible concern to a God
who cares for His people's total welfare (17 : 1–26 : 19).
Blessings and cursings are then listed in a closing passage
of some length (27 : 1–30 : 20). If we carefully examine
the message of this book, we shall soon discover
that the leading ideas are gathered around *four key
words*:

(i) *Remember*. This word invites the children of Israel
to look over their shoulders and view the past. They are
told not to forget that God has done great things for
them. You will remember that this forms the basic
theme in the introductory four chapters of *Deuteronomy* (4 : 32), and it also recurs throughout the main
section of the book. The people of God have always
treasured an acute sense of history and, by reflecting on
the past, the believing community has been encouraged
to step out into the unknown future. Therefore, 'remember' is a most important word in *Deuteronomy*
(5 : 15; 7 : 18; 8 : 2, 18; 9 : 7, 27; 15 : 15; 16 : 3, 12; 24 : 9,
18; 25 : 17). It is a key-word for the Christian life too:
'You shall remember that *you* were a servant . . . and
the Lord *your* God brought *you* out . . . with a mighty
hand and an outstretched arm' (5 : 15). All too easily we
can lapse into the sin of careless ingratitude. We too
forget the wonderful things that God has done for us in
Christ.

(ii) *Love*. This is the next key-word in the book. The

foundations of this immense biblical theme are found in
God's love for us. The apostle John realised that in the
Christian life we do not find a starting-point in our love
for God (1 John 4 : 10, 19). We can only love because we
have first been loved. *Deuteronomy* points out the shattering truth that He does not love the children of Israel
because of their numerical strength (7 : 7) but just because He wants to love them. Look up the references
and notice the supreme place that is given to this theme
—5 : 10; 6 : 5; 7 : 7, 9, 13; 10 : 12, 15, 18, 19; 11 : 1, 13, 22;
13 : 3; 15 : 16; 19 : 9; 30 : 6, 16, 20. When you have
studied these references you will see that the theme is
developed in this obvious way—God loves us; we should
love Him in return; we ought to express that love for
Him by loving others, especially the needy and unwanted people in society. The Hebrew passion for good
works arose directly out of their lofty doctrine of God.
Their belief in Him affected their behaviour towards
others. We ought to note also that this word often trans-
lated as 'steadfast love' in the RSV is the best we can do
in English with a rich Hebrew word ('hesed') which
means covenant-love, loyal-love, love between parties
who are linked together in an enduring bond of partnership and dependence.

(iii) *Beware.* This warning-word appears in an important context in *Deuteronomy.* The people are told
that, once they settle in an already prosperous land,
they will want to make it more prosperous. But they are
told that material prosperity and godly living do not
always make good companions. The appeal of this book
is not only to *remember* God's goodness in the past, but
beware (RSV 'take heed') lest we forget Him in the
present. (4 : 9, 23; 6 : 12; 8 : 11, 14, 19; 9 : 7). Riches bring
their special perils with them. The Lord God warned His

people that when possessions increase men often forget their gracious Giver. This is a warning few of us can ignore in our own day. If God seems to withhold certain things from us perhaps He knows that we will be far better Christians without them!

(iv) *Obey*. The fourth word focuses attention on our glad response to the revealed will of God. He has made Himself known to us through His Word; our part is to do what He asks. You will remember that, in introducing this particular book, we have already mentioned the near-eastern treaty pattern. The king who made this treaty demanded total obedience. If the monarch making the treaty agreed to obey, blessing would follow. If he ignored these claims and broke his treaty-promises, then a curse was pronounced upon him and his wayward nation. 'Obey' is a key term and is often found throughout *Deuteronomy* (4:30; 8:20; 9:23; 13:4, 18; 15:5; 26:14, 17; 27:10; 28:1, 2, 15, 45, 62; 30:2). The same idea is expressed in the repeated 'Be careful' of the RSV (AV 'keep', RV 'observe')—5:32; 6:3, 25; 7:11; 8:1; 11:22, 32; 12:1, 32; 15:5; 17:10; 19:9; 24:8; 28:1, 15, 58.

These four words summarise *Deuteronomy's* central message—remember, love, beware and obey.

3. GOD'S SERVANTS (Chapters 31–34)

The closing chapters of this magnificent book direct our thoughts to two servants of God. Moses is nearing the end of his days and he knows full well that his opportunities of service are fast declining (31:1, 2). Joshua is therefore appointed as his successor. God never leaves Himself without a witness. In His mercy He gives well-earned rest to those whose task is complete, and thrusts new responsibilities on those who follow in their steps.

In his *Pilgrims Progress*, John Bunyan captured this theme as he described the moment when Mr. Valiant for Truth was about to cross the river. The courageous pilgrim had finished his work and, addressing his friends, he said: 'I am going to my Father's; and though with great difficulty I have got hither, yet now I do not repent me of all the troubles I have been at to arrive where I am. My sword I give to him that shall succeed me in my pilgrimage and my courage and skill to him who can get it. My marks and scars I carry with me, to be a witness for me that I have fought His battles who now will be my rewarder.'

This was such a moment for Moses. His sword of truth was handed to Joshua, and though that old Valiant for Truth was not allowed to cross the Jordan River which lay ahead, he entered into his promised rest. God loved him so much that He personally took over the funeral arrangements (34 : 5, 6). But before the old warrior took leave of his troublesome congregation he left with them some great truths about the unchanging God. The final chapters of *Deuteronomy* record his parting address to the assembled people. The portraiture of God found in these passages is among some of the most priceless treasures of the Old Testament. He is the God who strides out in front of His people, preparing the way ahead (31 : 3). He stands by our side when troubles assail us (31 : 6–8, 23), and is the Rock beneath our feet when we feel that everything else is slipping away (32 : 4, 15, 18, 30, 31). He has been patient with us, like an eagle training her young to fly (32 : 11, 12) and He is, at one and the same time, like a fortress around us and strong arms beneath us (33 : 27). No wonder those who rely on Him are truly happy (33 : 29). It was with this kind of spiritual

confidence that Moses had journeyed with a discon-
tented multitude through a dreary wilderness, and
it was with that same deep assurance that Joshua was
commissioned to continue God's work.

A Captain and His Invincible Commander

OUR study of *Deuteronomy* finished with reference to a simple ceremony in which Moses handed over his leadership responsibilities to Joshua. The book which bears the new leader's name records the continuing story of the people of God, their arrival at the river Jordan and their entry into and conquest of the prosperous land of Canaan. *Deuteronomy* ended with an account of the burial of Moses; *Joshua* opens with God's rousing call to that great man's successor: 'Moses my servant is dead; now therefore arise, go over this Jordan, you and all this people, into the land which I am giving to them' (1:2). Once again, we notice that while we are studying *history* we can perceive some great truths about *experience*. The book can be divided into three main sections:

1. OBSTACLES TO BE OVERCOME (Chapters 1–5)

Right at the beginning of this exciting story, Joshua is given clear instruction and rich encouragement: *Be confident* ('I will be with you; I will not fail you or forsake you', 1:5); *Be valiant* ('Be strong and of good courage', 1:6) and *Be attentive* ('being careful to do according to all the law', 1:7). Joshua realised that there were difficult situations ahead and unknown territories to be conquered but he was upheld by the assurance of God's presence: 'the Lord your God is with you wherever you go' (1 : 9).

The first five chapters of the book relate the experiences of the children of Israel as they attempted to enter the land. There were immense obstacles which had to be overcome. A deep river blocked their way into the country which God had promised but they passed over it without difficulty (3 : 1–17) and marked this miraculous achievement by erecting a memorial to the praise of their unfailing God (4 : 1–24). The stones at Gilgal were to proclaim God's deliverance to generations then unborn. Just as their children at Passover time enquired, 'What do you mean by this service?' (Exod. 12 : 26), so children of later generations would say 'What do these stones mean?' (4 : 21). The Passover feast marked the moment of their deliverance at the beginning of the journey; the Gilgal stones testified to their deliverance at its close. But there were other problems ahead. The river was behind them, but the well-fortified cities were ahead. They could not easily be captured. Spies had been sent to view Jericho (2 : 1–24) and the men who had gone on that dangerous errand returned in the spirit of optimistic confidence (2 : 24).

Knowing the hazards to come, Joshua celebrated the Passover and ensured that the covenant-sign of circumcision was given its proper place in their religious life (5 : 1–10). Now that the Israelites could enjoy the rich provisions of their new land, the daily manna ceased (5 : 11, 12). At this dramatic moment, with unconquered territories on the horizon, Joshua had an unexpected encounter with a divine Messenger (5 : 13–15). The man's sword was drawn and he described himself to Joshua as 'commander of the army of the Lord' (5 : 14). Surely this was none other than the Lord Himself, manifesting Himself in human form specially for the encouragement of the new leader. Joshua now realised that every time he went out to battle, he could count on the unseen help of this mighty Victor. No wonder he fell on his knees and worshipped. Any obstacle could be overcome if this God was by his side. We too can triumph over our spiritual enemies, knowing that the Lord who helped Joshua is with us too. (Matt. 28:20, John 16:33).

2. ENEMIES TO BE VANQUISHED (Chapters 6–12)

For many days the gates of Jericho had been firmly barred. Its citizens were terrified as they looked from their firm walls and saw the Israelite host camping on the plain. Despite its strength, the city was easily taken. God was on their side. Only Rahab and her family were saved. She had done what was commanded by the spies and the scarlet cord had been hung from her window; obedience to the word had brought safety to her household. Later generations of believing people remembered the story and drew lessons from it about the salvation that God has promised to all (Heb. 11:31, James 2:25, 26). But although the harlot Rahab obeyed the word spoken to her, one pathetic man in the Israelite camp did not. Rahab's obedience brought salvation to others (2:18, 19; 6:22, 23) but Achan's disobedience brought death upon his fellows (7:1–5). All the Hebrew soldiers had been told that everything taken in the capture of Jericho must be devoted to the Lord (6:17–21), but Achan had stolen an attractive robe, some silver and gold, and buried the loot in his tent. His sin was exposed and had to be judged; the Israelites were made to realise that God's orders were always for their good and what He commanded must be obeyed (7:6–26). The following chapters tell of the various conquests of Joshua and his armies. It was a well-organised campaign. Once the cities of Jericho and Ai had been taken (6:1–8:35) the land was thereby divided into two distinct sections and unified resistance by the Canaanites had been made almost impossible. The Israelite soldiers first subdued the southern part of the country (10:1–43), and then went on to conquer the northern territories (11:1–23). An impressive list of Joshua's victories brings this part of the book to a close (12:1–24).

3. POSSESSIONS TO BE ENJOYED (Chapters 13–24)

The remaining chapters of *Joshua* are given over to various details regarding the division of land among the different tribes (13:1–19:51), the establishment of six cities of refuge for the protection of anyone who accidentally killed one of their fellow-countrymen (20:1–9, cf. Num. 35:9–34, Deut. 19:1–10), the allocation of forty-eight cities among the Levites (21:1–45, cf. 13:33; Num. 35:1–8), and the settlement of some tribes on the eastern side of the country (22:1–34). Just as *Deuteronomy* had closed with a farewell message from Moses (Deut. 32:1–33:29) so *Joshua* ends with a final address from Moses' gifted successor. His message is in the form of two addresses. In the first (23:1–16) he reminds the people of the continuing help of the divine Commander who had met him on the plain of Jericho (23:3, 5, 9, 10) and brought them all to victory. This is what the Lord had done for them. Some key-words then summarized his message about their responsibility to Him: *Keep* (23:6) and do all that is written; *Cleave* to the Lord as much in the future as you have in the past (23:8); *Love* Him, and show your love by refusing to worship the many idols of your new land and by making sure that you do not marry one of the heathen Canaanites

(23:11). Interestingly enough, the last address which Joshua gave seems to follow the treaty-pattern which we noticed in *Deuteronomy*: *God's achievements* (24:1–13) *are recalled*, then *God's demands are declared* (24:14–18) and *God's people are warned* (24:19–28). Joshua died, and Israel lost one of its greatest leaders (24:29–33).

The message of *Joshua* is a really important one for our Christian lives. There are three great themes which constantly appear in one form or another throughout the book—faithfulness, purity and victory. The story of Israel's conquest is told so as to reaffirm our confidence in a God who is faithful, holy and invincible. We can best observe these features of the book if we express them in this simple form:

(i) God's people can depend on Him

Throughout the centuries God has repeatedly told His servants that one day they would enter the land of Canaan and make it their own (Gen. 13:15–17; 15:7, 18–21; 17:8; 26:2–5; 28:13–14; 48:21; 50:24, 25; Exod. 3:8). His word is utterly dependable. He never lets His people down. This great truth is repeated throughout *Joshua*. Look up 11:23; 21:43–45; 23:14. Joshua's final testimony was that 'not one thing has failed of all the good things which the Lord your God promised'. He has made these great promises to us and will not fail us either.

(ii) God's people must listen to Him

The plea for holiness runs all the way through this book, just as it does through *Leviticus*. Those who want to please God must live as He desires – in purity and obedience. This is why the treasures of Jericho had to be offered to the Lord. God knew that these possessions would create a wrong sense of values in the minds of the people; they were best 'devoted' entirely to the Lord's work (6 : 17–19). This would ensure a right understanding of spiritual priorities and avoid the perils of greed, jealousy and rivalry among the people. The Israelites were clearly told right from the start that these encounters were God's battles and, if they wished to conquer, they must be clean before Him (3 : 5; 7 : 11–13). The holiness He demanded was not a vague religious concept; it was intensely practical. It meant that the people were neither to offer their adoration to idols, nor their love to unbelievers. Both could eventually rob them of their love for God and His people (23 : 7, 12; 24 : 14–15, 23). These truths are reiterated in the New Testament (1 Thess. 1 : 9; 1 John 5 : 21; 2 Cor. 6 : 14; 7 : 1). We are also engaged in a fight and, if we would conquer, we too must be clean (2 Tim. 2 : 3–5, 20–22; 4 : 7; Eph. 6 : 10–18).

(iii) *God's people are saved by Him*

The truth of salvation is enshrined in the very name given to the Israelite leader at this time. Joshua simply means 'Jehovah is Salvation' and is the Old Testament form of the familiar New Testament name 'Jesus'. The exciting story told in this book is an encouragement to all believers that Jesus, the divine Commander, is by their side (5 : 13–15) and in His strength victory is assured. The conquest of Canaan did not come about solely because of good planning, military insight and careful strategy (24 : 11–13). These things obviously played their part, but the victory was due to two great factors—God's promise and God's presence. He has said that He will deliver us in time of trial and accompany us through all the experiences of life. Those who, through personal faith in Christ, have trusted in His saving achievement upon the Cross and have acknowledged His Lordship over their lives, are assured that He will fight with them and continually bring them to victory (Rom. 8:31–39; 1 Cor. 15:57; 2 Cor. 2:14; 2 Tim. 4:17).

Doing What we Like

BEFORE Joshua took leave of the people he gave them a serious warning about idolatry and mixed marriages (Joshua 23 : 11–15; 24 : 14, 23). Indeed, it seems to have been more of an exhortation than a warning for some of them already had strange gods (24 : 23) and possibly unbelieving wives also. The next book in the Bible library opens with the sad tale of this kind of compromise with the Canaanite enemy. Moses had explained that the occupants of the land must be driven out if God's people wanted to be assured of peace (Exod. 23 : 32, 33; 34 : 12–16; Num. 33 : 55; Deut. 7 : 1–5). *Judges* is the story of what happens when men only partially obey Him (1 : 19, cf. Joshua 17 : 16–18). It is an account of what follows incomplete surrender, when men do what they like rather than what they are told. A key phrase in *Judges* is found in two passages towards the end of the book. We shall look at it now in order to get a clear picture of the spiritual meaning and the contemporary significance of this book : 'Every man did what was right in his own eyes' (17:6; 21:25). Expediency became more important than obedience and throughout the opening chapter of Judges there is a constantly repeated statement : 'Manasseh did not drive out the inhabitants . . . but the Canaanites persisted in dwelling in that land' and it was the same with Ephraim, Zebulun, Asher and Napthali (1 : 27–33). The second chapter opens with the divine indictment, 'You have

D

not obeyed my command' (2:2). Instead of possessing the land and enjoying its fruits, many of the Israelites had been driven from their homes and lived in fear of their lives (1:34–35). *Judges* narrates the sequence of events which followed this incomplete victory, and it has a series of obvious lessons for our own lives. We do not always enjoy the peace and prosperity that the Lord has promised because we do not do exactly what He commands. Total obedience is as much a key-theme in the New Testament as in the Old (John 2:5; 14:15; 15:10; Acts 5:29; 6:7; Rom. 6:16, 17; Phil. 2:12; Heb. 5:9; 1 Pet. 1:14, 22).

Judges follows a cyclic pattern, a summary of which is found in 2:11–23. The Israelite people forsake God and, in their disobedience, give themselves over to idolatry. In order to discipline them, God forsakes them and leaves them in the cruel hands of their enemies. Desperate about their plight, they cry to the Lord for help and he delivers them by raising up a 'judge' to lead them to victory. However, once given a period of peace and prosperity, they again forsake the Lord and the pattern is repeated. The book records the various exploits of these military leaders and as the pages are turned we read about Othniel (3:7–11), Ehud (3:12–30), Shamgar (3:31), Deborah and Barak (4:1–5:31), Gideon (6:1–8:32) Tola and Jair (10:1–5), Jephthah (10:6–12:7), Ibzan (12:8–10), Elon (12:11–12), Abdon (12:13–15) and Samson (13:1–16:31).

The material thus far has obviously focused on battle-fields and conquests but the closing chapters of the book (17:1–21:25) give a vivid yet distressing account of the moral, religious and social conditions of the time. It shows us just what happens when a nation forgets God and insists on going its own way. Some of the stories here have a clear warning for our own time. They tell of greed and avarice (17 : 1–3), idolatry and disobedience (17 : 4–13). Imagine a Levite (Num. 8 : 5–19) agreeing to serve as a priest in a home where forbidden idols were treasured (Exod. 20 : 4–5)! The story continues with horrific examples of self-seeking, disloyalty, plunder and theft (18 : 1–31). The people of the land had become heartless and selfish (18 : 7; 19 : 15, 18), immoral and cruel (19 : 16–26). Domestic strife spreads until it borders on civil war; violence and aggression rob the land of peace. The country which 'flowed with milk and honey' became a place of bloodshed and bitterness. All this selfishness and strife is summed up in the sad words with which the book closes: 'every man did what was right in his own eyes' (21 : 25).

What is this sad book saying to us today? It tells us that disobedience to God brings distress upon men. When God gives orders He does not do it because He wants to inhibit men but because He wants to enrich them. He knows what is right and good and best for us. In our self-centredness, we cannot always see the issues of life clearly. Only in obeying His voice shall we enjoy His gifts.

But we must not let the general sadness of this story rob us of some glorious insights into spiritual loyalty and valiant conflict on the part of some of Israel's judges at this time. A number of great truths become obvious as we read their story carefully. *Judges* does not only tell us about the wickedness of men. It also declares the goodness of God. Three aspects of God's nature stand out particularly.

1. GOD'S JUSTICE

The book opens with the story of the successful encounter of the tribes of Judah and Simeon with the heathen king, Adoni-bezek. He had been terribly cruel to his enemies over the years and the same punishment which he inflicted upon seventy different kings came to him also in the moment of his capture (1 : 1–7). He recognised that God had requited him for his harsh treatment of others. No man can hope to be cruel to others and get away with it; ultimately, God's judgment will come upon all heartless people.

2. GOD'S POWER

The secret of power in the lives of the various judges is that God transformed the lives of ordinary men, cowardly men, inept men, and made them into fit channels for His immense power. It is extremely interesting to see that in several places in the book special emphasis is laid either on the physical inadequacy or the simple military equipment of the conquerors. Ehud was left-handed (3 : 15); Shamgar went to battle with only an ox-goad as a weapon (3 : 31). Although there must have been several mighty men in Israel, two women were used to bring the people to victory (4 : 1–5 : 31). Gideon was quite a coward, terrified at the prospect of meeting the Midianites, until God took control of his life (6 : 11–40). Samson used a jaw-bone of an ass in warfare (15 : 15), and this last of the judges wrought his greatest victory when he was blind and helpless (16 : 25–30). What was the secret of their strength? *Judges* has quite a lot to say about the Holy Spirit. 'The Spirit of the Lord came upon' Othniel (3 : 10), Gideon (6 : 34), Jephthah (11 : 29) and Samson (13 : 25; 14 : 6, 19; 15 : 14). These men had been chosen by God for difficult assignments and, in order to equip them for hazardous tasks, God's Spirit came to take possession of them. The word used in 6:34 actually means that the Spirit 'clothed Himself' with Gideon, the fearful man He had chosen for courageous service. He filled such men with His own power and wore their frail flesh almost like a robe. In the Old Testament the Holy Spirit came to indwell men for limited periods and for special tasks, while in the New He comes to live in the hearts of *all* who obey Him (Acts 5:32) and for *all* time.

3. GOD'S GRACE

Judges is not a record of unblemished devotion, far from it. There are stories here of people who made serious mistakes. Gideon brought disaster among the people because of his avarice (8:24–27), Jephthah brought heartache into his family circle because of his rash words (11:30–40). It was easy to talk about sacrificing when he did not think it would cost him much personally. After all, a slave was easily replaced, but it was different with a daughter. He ought never to have said such a thing. Human sacrifice was forbidden. Samson similarly brought heartache first to his godly parents, and eventually to the entire nation, because of his sensuality and arrogance. Jephthah made a vow he should not have made; Samson made one and did not keep it (13:3–5, 7). Yet, despite these details of human failure, the overall picture encourages the reader to trust in a God who takes the weak and makes them strong, who comes to the fallen and raises them up. Samson's story is the most striking illustration of this glorious principle. Bound in fetters, grinding corn in a prison-house, trapped in all the sadness and darkness of remorse, what hope is there for such a man? His hope is in God. In a moment of venturesome faith, he cries for help (16:28–30). It was not his first experience of prayer (15:18, 19) but his spirits were now at their lowest ebb. Yet, even in his weakness, he refused to believe that God would continue to hold his sin against him. His flowing hair had once been an outward symbol of a dedicated man and it had been cut by a woman who was paid to degrade him (16:4–21). One of the most wonderful verses in the whole book is that which follows the account of his pathetic failure. It enshrines a spiritual principle: 'But the hair of his head began to grow again after it had been shaved' (16:22). If we are truly penitent, God delights to forgive. If we cast ourselves upon Him, we may accomplish more after our failures than we ever did before them (16:30). He always deals with His children in grace.

A Refugee's Reward

In our Bible-library we have been looking at some
weighty volumes. We now come to an important work
which is little more than a tract or pamphlet. It goes by
the name of one of its principal characters, *Ruth*. The
story follows *Judges* in order and probably belongs to
the same period of history as that covered by the closing
chapters of that book. A Bethlehemite married-couple
named Elimelech and Naomi left the famine-stricken
territory of Judah with their two boys and sought refuge
in the land of Moab. Elimelech eventually died and his
sons married Moabite women. Ten years later further
grief came to the family circle in that both husbands
died so that these two Moabite wives, Orpah and
Ruth, shared the loneliness of their mother-in-law. In
her increased agony Naomi longed for home. She had
lost husband and sons: only her friends were left, and
they were miles away in Bethlehem. Her home-land was
now free from famine so, determined to return to Judah,
Naomi began her long journey accompanied by her
daughters-in-law. She was going home, but Orpah and
Ruth were travelling to an unknown, perhaps even hostile, land. Naomi begged the widows to stay in their
home-country and marry again. Orpah took her advice
but, in memorable words of rich beauty, Ruth insisted on
staying by Naomi's side. She was not only attracted to
her mother-in-law as a person; she was drawn to her
faith (1 : 1–18).

The two homeless women came eventually to Bethlehem and it was the beginning of barley-harvest (1:19–
22). Under the compassionate rules of the Mosaic Law,
needy people were allowed to glean in the fields. Landowners were not allowed to remove every scrap of
grain from their harvest-fields. Some had to be left for
the poor (Lev. 19:9–10; 23:22) and a similar provision
was made for those who were in desperate need of oil
and fruit (Deut. 24:20–22). God loved the homeless and
poor so much that He framed His Law in such a way
that even a harvester's bad memory became a loving de-
vice for the care of His children (Deut. 24:19). The law
said that such gleanings were for widows and sojourners
and the two women certainly fell within these categories
of need. Ruth went to work. She did her part; God did
His. She was a stranger in Bethlehem and one field was
as good as another, but God guided her to part of a field
which belonged to Naomi's kinsman, Boaz (2:1–7). The
kinsman-idea was another loving provision by God for
the care of families in distress. By these laws, Israelites
accepted definite obligations for the care of deprived
members of their family-circle. Although she did not
know it, Ruth started to glean in the field of Boaz and
thus started a series of happy events which ultimately
led to her marriage (2:8–4:13). Her child was to be the
grandfather of great King David (4:14–22).

This little story reads well after the tragic incidents
recorded in *Judges*. There may be a host of reasons why
it is found in Holy Scripture, but one of them must be
mentioned here. The central theme is surely this: *Put
God first*. Those who honour Him, He will honour (1
Sam. 2:30). Orphah did the natural thing and looked
after her own interests (1:14, 15) but Ruth did the
costly thing and stayed alongside her needy mother-in-

law. Moreover, she put her trust in God (1 : 16–18) even though, at that time, it did not seem to pagans as though He cared much about His people. Famine had driven a godly couple from Judah, and a triple bereavement was driving the widow back. A family of four had left in search of food; one solitary soul was now returning in search of comfort, something more precious than bread. But Ruth had begun to realise that Naomi's faith had been her only anchor in times of trouble and she wanted that kind of confidence and peace. Putting God first, she joined her widowed companion and promised to stay with her until the end (1 : 17). Such devotion is always rewarded. Boaz said that to her in fact as she worked in his fields : 'The Lord recompense you for what you have done, and a full reward be given you by the Lord, the God of Israel, under whose wings you have come to take refuge' (2 : 12). How wonderfully He rewarded Ruth for her loving service. The unfolding story tells how God did reward her, and possibly hints at some of the ways in which He may choose to reward us for unselfish devotion and fidelity. No believer works simply for reward, of course, but it is a fact of experience that God chooses to give it. In Ruth's case :

1. HE ENLARGED HER HORIZONS

Moabite religion had obviously meant little to her but she was at least surrounded by friends and acquaintances in Moab. It was a risky thing to go into another country (cf. 2 : 22). After all, Naomi might not live for long anyway; this would have been a natural way to reason. But because she denied herself and put her trust in a God who cares, life became far more wonderful for her than it could ever have been in Moab. She took refuge under God's wings (2 : 12) and He in turn opened up an entirely

new and joyous life for her. He will do the same for us
if we put our trust in Him.

2. HE GUIDED HER STEPS

The day Ruth left their simple lodging in Bethlehem,
she had no idea where to go. All the fields looked alike,
but the narrator says 'she happened to come to the part
of the field belonging to Boaz' (2 : 3). As she surveyed the
different fields, God was directing her. Things do not
happen to believers by chance. He loves to guide us
(Rom. 8 : 28. Prov. 3 : 5, 6). Her great-grandson was later
to express the truth in memorable words: 'The steps of
a man are from the Lord' (Psa. 37 : 23).

3. HE MET HER NEEDS

The two women were hungry. When Naomi had left
Judah years before there was no food for anybody. Now
there was plenty, but she had no money to buy it. What
a glorious thing that God thought that problem out long
before she experienced it (Lev. 19 : 9–10). Men and
women down the centuries have proved, with Naomi
and Ruth, that He does not choose to leave His children
destitute. Years later, in a time of personal trouble,
Ruth's great-grandson was to compose a psalm of confidence and triumph, and gladly sing: 'Those who seek
the Lord lack no good thing' (Psa. 34 : 10). He does provide for all who come to Him.

4. HE INCREASED HER JOYS

Ruth left Moab a heart-broken widow. It was all so
tragic, but how good God is. Within a year or so her
dreary future was gloriously changed and she held her
new-born baby in her arms. Since that decisive moment
when she openly declared her simple trust in Naomi's

God she had been given spiritual confidence, shelter, food, love, home and now family. God is no man's debtor. Jesus once said that those who put God's kingdom first will find that all the other things of life fall into their right and proper place. 'All these things shall be yours as well' (Matt. 6:33, Rom. 8:32). This is what the book of Ruth is all about.

Give Us a King

WE come now to two books which in the original Hebrew Bible formed a single volume—the *Books of Samuel*. We have become accustomed to classify this kind of biblical literature as 'historical books' but the Jewish people themselves described them as 'the former prophets'. They obviously believed that God was speaking as clearly through the historical events we have already considered (*Joshua–Judges*) as through the prophetic books we have yet to study. So, the books from *Joshua* through to *2 Kings* became known as 'the former prophets', whereas later prophetic records were gathered together under the title of 'the latter prophets'. Our immediate purpose is to look at the story as it unfolds in what we now call *1 and 2 Samuel*. This twin-volume begins by telling us about the leadership of the last two judges; it goes on to tell us about the nation's first two kings. The leading characters in chronological order are Eli, Samuel, Saul and David. The historical narrative can, therefore, be divided in this way:

1. THE LAST JUDGES (1 Samuel Chapters 1–7)

In its closing chapters the *Book of Judges* frequently observes that 'in those days there was no king in Israel' (Judges 17:6; 18:1; 19:1; 21:25). The first seven chapters of *1 Samuel* give us an account of life under two judges, Eli and Samuel. These two men officiated mainly as priest and prophet respectively, but they obviously held positions of leadership which extended far beyond their specific religious duties.

(i) *Eli*

Eli's leadership (1 : 1–4 : 22) does not appear to have been either spiritually or morally healthy. The priest himself was devout but he seems to have lacked all sense of parental responsibility. Both his sons were worthless men who had 'no regard for the Lord' (2 : 12). The grim story of materialistic greed (2 : 12–17), moral degradation (2 : 22–25), spiritual bankruptcy (3 : 1), religious superstition (4 : 3), national distress (4 : 2, 10) and domestic grief (4 : 13–21) is only relieved by the moving account of Hannah's earnest prayer and God's gracious answer to it (1 : 1–28). This devout woman longed for a child and, in due time, her boy was born. His grateful mother's song of thanksgiving (2 : 1–10) has much in common with the exultant song of the Virgin Mary (Luke 1 : 46–55) and it is an interesting study to set these passages alongside each other and compare them. Perhaps young Mary knew these words very well; they certainly formed the spiritual background for her own praise and gratitude.

(ii) *Samuel*

After Eli's tragic death (4 : 18) the responsibility for Israelite affairs came into the hands of Samuel (5 : 1–7 : 17). The period had begun with Philistine oppression. The Ark of the Covenant, an outward symbol of God's presence among His people, had been captured, but it brought disaster upon one Philistine city after another. At the end of seven months they longed to get rid of it, and so they set it on a cart drawn by two cows who im-

mediately took their precious cargo back into Israelite
territory (5:1–7:2). Samuel used the occasion to call
the people to a renewed faith in God. They confessed
their sins and throughout the remaining years of
Samuel's leadership were victorious over their Philistine
oppressors (7:3–17).

2. THE FIRST KINGS (1 Samuel Chapter 8 to
2 Samuel Chapter 24)

But although Samuel's public life was entirely satis-
factory, his home circumstances were far from good. He
had walked with God, but tragically enough, his two
sons 'did not walk in his ways, but turned aside after
gain; they took bribes and perverted justice' (8:3). The
grief of Eli had repeated itself in the life of his servant.
The people knew that Samuel's corrupt sons must not be
given positions of national responsibility, so they begged
for a king. Samuel was not happy about the idea, and
warned them of its dangers, but finally acquiesced (8:4–
22). The sad feature about the request was that the
people wanted a king so as to be like their heathen neighbours (8:5, 20). It was an indication of declining spirituality. Deeply committed believers are not mere copyists.
Other people's practices are not their guide; they prefer
to ask whether their actions will be pleasing to God.

(i) Saul

The person chosen as first king was Saul, a tall, hand-
some and shy man of great promise (9:1–2; 10:20–23).
He did not want to rule (9:21; 10:21–22) but, once
acknowledged as king, he made an excellent beginning.
He knew how to control his tongue (10:25–27) and how
to rally his people (11:1–15). Samuel pleaded with the

new king and his subjects to follow after God (12 : 1–18)
and he promised to pray earnestly for them (12 : 19–25).
But it was not long before the prophet began to suspect
Saul's devotion. In a moment of impatience the new
king took it upon himself to offer the ritualistic sacrifices instead of waiting for Samuel, and he was clearly
told of his error (13 : 1–15). Later stories reveal his hasty
temper (14 : 24–45), his avarice (15 : 9), hypocrisy
(15 : 13) and disobedience (15 : 17–23). He became totally
unsuitable for kingship and Samuel told him so (15 : 24–
34). David, the youngest son of a Bethlehemite was
secretly anointed as Saul's successor (16 : 1–13) and was
later employed as a musician at Saul's court (16 : 14–23).
An astonishing victory over a Philistine warrior made
him famous overnight (17 : 1–58). Saul's son developed
a deep affection for David, but Saul became extremely
jealous of his popularity and the young victor had to
escape to safety. The king then developed a serious
neurosis and tried everything within his power to slay
David (18 : 1–20 : 42). Anyone who did anything to help
David was also in danger and the fugitive had to get his
own family out of the country (21 : 1–22 : 23). Gathering
a group of men around him, David engaged in various
conflicts with the Philistines and yet on other occasions
sought refuge in their country.

While staying at the Philistine court David led a number of military expeditions against the enemies of Israel,
and all the time the Philistine king thought he had been
fighting against Israel itself (23 : 1–28 : 2). About this
time the prophet Samuel died. At the time of this
national and personal distress Saul asked a witch to communicate with the dead prophet, but the sad message she
received told of Saul's imminent downfall (28 : 3–25).
Eventually David had to leave the Philistine camp

(29 : 1–11), only to return to a tragic situation in Israel in which the homes of his compatriots had been burnt and their women and children carried away. David's wives also were among the captives and, in their anger, his soldiers talked of stoning him. They naturally blamed him for taking them away from their home responsibilities (30 : 1–6), but David pursued the raiders and saved every one of the prisoners (30 : 7–31). In the ensuing battle against the Philistines, Saul and his son Jonathan were both killed (31 : 1–13).

(ii) *David*

The second book of *Samuel* covers most of the reign of David. It begins with his lament over the death of Saul and Jonathan; this famous 'song of the bow' reveals his affection for his friend and his loyalty to his king (1 : 17–27). David had never given Saul any reason for jealousy; his fidelity to the king was a model of courageous devotion and honour.

Saul had another son, Ishbosheth, who had obvious pretensions to kingship. The opening chapters of 2 *Samuel* (2 : 1–4 : 12) expose the conflicting loyalties throughout the nation; some were for David, others preferred to keep the dynasty in Saul's family. Ishbosheth was supported by his forceful captain, Abner, who soon realised he was fighting a losing battle. After a domestic quarrel, Abner decided that it might be best to go over to David's side so he met David to discuss peace terms. When Joab, David's captain, heard of their meeting he murdered Abner in order to avenge the death of Asahel, his brother, who had earlier been killed by Abner. Ishbosheth was then assassinated by two brothers who thought this would win them a place in David's favour. In fact, the king was terribly grieved that they had murdered a member of Saul's house while he was not in a position to defend himself, and both the murderers were slain. This series of desperately unhappy events illustrates a principle frequently evident in the Old Testament yet sometimes overlooked by those who read it. Sin is frightening and horrible because of the subtle way in which it reproduces itself. Transgression is rarely an isolated phenomena; one sin soon gives birth to another. There is little that can be done to halt the awful process. The inevitable chain-reaction can only be broken when a believer allows God to invade his life with a power, forgiveness and grace sufficient to let sin die within him. In this way the self-perpetuating sinful process is broken. This is what it means to die to sin.

With the death of both Abner and Ishbosheth the previously divided tribes gave their total allegiance to David (5:1–5). The city of Jerusalem, formerly a Jebusite stronghold, was captured by David and his troops (5:6–10), who were also successful in an encounter against the Philistines (5:11–25). David wanted to bring the ark to Jerusalem but his servants carelessly ignored the Word of God and, disregarding the injunction that it should always be carried with the aid of staves, placed it on a cart (6:1–6). Disaster followed and the people knew that they had grieved God (6:7–9). The ark was left in the near-by house of Obed-edom and all the time it was there the man who had sheltered the ark greatly prospered (6:10–11). The king regarded this as a sign of divine pardon and renewed favour and the ark was then carried to Jerusalem amidst scenes of exuberant rejoicing on the part of both king and people (6:12–19). David's wife, Michal, was not in sympathy with his spiritual enthusiasm and despised him for his participation in this religious procession (6:20–23, cf. Matt.

E

10:36). David wanted to build a 'permanent home' for the ark of God but was told that his son would be given that privilege (7:1–29).

Accounts are given of various military exploits (8:1–10:19) and we then read a tragic story which further illustrates the principle that sin inevitably reproduces itself (11:1–27). Perhaps it all started with David's idleness (11:1). Bathsheba was not free from blame (11:2). Joab became dangerously involved (11:14–17) and an innocent officer, Uriah, was cruelly slain. Nathan, a courageous prophet, skilfully exposed David's sin and divine punishment followed (12:1–23). This sad event was quickly followed by further trouble in his home. David's immorality and cruelty was copied by his son, Amnon (13:1–19) and the incidents which followed further illustrate the 'exceeding sinfulness of sin'. Amnon was slain by Absalom, another of David's sons, and the murderer was forced to flee from the royal palace (13:20–39). By a subtle and typical plot, Joab procured Absalom's return (14:1–33) but that was only the beginning of more serious trouble for David. Once reinstated at the royal court, Absalom began to enlist personal support, engender disaffection for David, and secretly plot a rebellion (15:1–12). The dispirited king thought it in the nation's best interests to leave Jerusalem rather than bring disaster to the city and its people (15:13–37). A fascinating spy story follows (16:1–17:23) and, thanks to this successful piece of espionage, David and his companions crossed over the Jordan to safety (17:24–29). A battle ensues, though David is no longer strong enough to participate in warfare himself. In the fierce military encounter the soldiers entered a wood and Absalom was caught in the branches of an oak tree by his long hair and later killed by Joab despite David's command that his life be spared (18 : 1–15).

The king was broken-hearted over the death of his rebellious son (18 : 16–19 : 10) but eventually returned to the capital city (19 : 11–20 : 3). Another minor revolution had to be quelled (20 : 1–26) followed quickly by a period of famine and further warfare (21 : 1–22). The final chapters record one of David's many songs of thanksgiving (22 : 1–51 cf. Psa. 18 : 2–50), his last words (23 : 1–7), a list of his trusted warriors (23 : 8–39) with a closing touch of irony by the deliberate mention of the last name (23 : 39)—a loyal man commissioned to protect David, who died at the hand of his own king; such are the ways of sinners. David's census of Israel and the ensuing disaster (24 : 1–25) bring the book to a close.

The *Books of Samuel* record a long story. We have already noted that one of its main lessons is one which is also illustrated in other parts of the Old Testament, that once we sin we release a destructive sinister power over which we have no further control. As we close our study of these twin-volumes we must briefly consider the four main characters who emerge at successive periods in this unfolding story. Their lives have many lessons, but we single out one important one in each case. The early chapters of *1 Samuel* introduce us to *Eli*, the priest. We can describe him as *a man whose weakness impaired his witness*. He ought to have corrected his immoral sons, but there were times when he seemed to have thought more of them than he thought of the Lord (1 Sam. 2 : 29). It is easy to be careless about our spiritual and moral responsibilities at home.

Then, in contrast, think about *Samuel*, the prophet. He was *a man whose obedience enriched his service*.

'Obedience' was a key word with Samuel. He observed the disobedience of the people (1 Sam. 8 : 19) and urged them to obey God's voice (12 : 14–15). He grieved over Saul's persistent disobedience (15 : 19, 20, 22), for he knew that though he had anointed him as king, a man with such a rebellious spirit could not possibly stay upon the throne of Israel. The prophet was sent to anoint Saul's successor and the narrative says '*Samuel did what the Lord commanded* and came to Bethlehem' (16 : 4). Do we do what the Lord commands?

Without doubt the most tragic figure in the book is Saul. He was *a man whose avarice corrupted his dedication*. He started out well, but greed and materialism invaded his thinking. 1 Sam. 15 is a pathetic account of the disobedient king's rejection of God's Word, and God's consequent rejection of him. Are we wasting our opportunities?

David is the character who dominates the book. He is not without his sins and mistakes, but the overall picture is that of a 'man after God's own heart' (1 Sam. 13 : 14). David went through a series of tragic experiences but the narratives in *1 and 2 Samuel* and some memorable psalms portray him as *a man whose adversities deepened his faith*. Study some of the narratives in *1 and 2 Samuel* with marginal references to psalms with historical titles, and notice how, in these trying circumstances, David cast himself upon the Lord and was sustained, e.g. 1 Sam. 19 : 11–12 (Psa. 59), 21 : 10–15 (Psa. 34). 'Abimelech' was possibly a title for a king of Gath, just as 'Pharaoh' was a title for an Egyptian ruler. This may account for the difference in name in 1 Sam. 21 : 10. Psa. 56 also refers to this occasion), 1 Sam. 24 : 1–7 (Psa. 142), 2 Sam. 12 : 1–15 (Psa. 51), 2 Sam. 15 : 13–17 (Psa. 3). These passages and the appropriate psalms indicate the depth of

David's devotion to the Lord and the help which was given to him during extremely perilous times. God will bring us through trouble if, like David, we cast ourselves upon Him.

Hollow Crowns

LIKE the *Books of Samuel*, the *First and Second Books of Kings* were originally one book in the Hebrew Bible. They continue the story of life under 'the kings' from the last few months of David's reign right down until the invasion of Jerusalem by the Babylonian armies, the destruction of its temple and the subsequent exile of its leading citizens. Once again, it is important for us to note that the vivid stories related in these books are not presented as *mere* history. What is here recorded is the unfolding story of the Hebrew kingdom as seen through the eyes of prophets. Almost as if to emphasise this, two great prophets dominate the story in the central section of the twin-volume, Elijah (1 Kings 17:1–2 Kings 1:18) and Elisha (2 Kings 2:1–13:20). Their presence at a crucial point in the narrative reminds us of the immense importance of the prophetic viewpoint in Hebrew religious life and thought. We must emphasise, therefore, that what is related here is *interpreted* history. Some kings are dismissed in a few verses, while the story of others occupies several chapters. We know, for example, that Omri, king of Israel, was one of their greatest rulers. Archaeological discoveries have revealed important details about his adventurous exploits and military successes, but the biblical account of his reign is dismissed in a few verses. The reason for this is quite simple; he may have been a successful monarch from a national and even international point of view, but from a spirit-

ual standpoint he was useless. 'Omri did what was evil
in the sight of the Lord' (1 Kings 16:25). What matters
is whether a man 'does what is right in the eyes of the
Lord' (e.g. 2 Kings 14:3); the historian regards little
else as worthy of mention. More than once, Shakespeare
commented on the hazards of kingship. Into the mouth
of Richard II he put these words:

> For within the hollow crown
> That rounds the temples of a mortal king
> Keeps death his court, and there the antic sits
> Scoffing his state and grinning at his pomp . . .
> Infusing him with self and vain conceit,
> As if this flesh which walls about our life
> Were brass impregnable.

As we trace the rise and fall of Hebrew rulers we may
well enter more deeply into the meaning of Shakespeare's incisive comments about the brief glory of
kings. Here and there in this story we read of a monarch
who led his people well, making it easy for them to
exercise faith in God and display love towards others.
But such enriching and inspiring stories are constantly
interrupted by tales of 'self and vain conceit'. Men arose
who could not manage their own lives, let alone control
a nation.

The constantly changing story in the *Books of Kings*
can be traced under three simple headings:

1. A DEPRIVED KINGDOM (1 Kings Chapters 1–11)
The closing events of David's long reign stand at the
beginning of the book, exposing all the usual bitter
controversies about succession (1:1–53). The old king

speaks his last words, not all edifying, (2 : 1–9), and Solomon then establishes himself as the new king by removing all possible opposition to his rule (2 : 13–46). The account of Solomon's reign has become strangely distorted in popular bible-story books and he is invariably portrayed as a fine exemplary figure endowed with superior wisdom, responsible for the construction of a magnificent temple, and greatly admired by all the kings and queens of surrounding nations. He did seek wisdom; that is perfectly true (3 : 1–28). He organised the life of the nation so that in the early part of his reign people were happy under his leadership (4 : 1–34). He also built a superb temple in Jerusalem (5 : 1–6 : 38), though we should note that he was almost twice as long building his own palace (compare 6 : 38 and 7 : 1, and remember that there were no chapter divisions when this book was first written). The newly constructed temple, its furnishing and its dedication are described in these chapters and Solomon's prayer is also recorded (7 : 1–8 : 66). But all this is only part of an otherwise depressing picture. The transition from David's rule to that of his son was not a particularly good one. It was the ordinary man in Israel who suffered most during the hard years when Solomon was on the throne. As his reign continued the people became seriously deprived of devout leadership, personal freedom and economic stability.

We have already observed in our study of the *Books of Samuel* that David's rule was not without its mistakes, but he did bring a rich *spiritual* contribution to the affairs of the nation. This cannot be said of Solomon. As so often happens, the longing for possessions displaced his concern about God. He disobeyed God's word about mixed marriages (3 : 1; 11 : 1–4), probably in order to strengthen his alliance with other nations, but it led to widespread idolatry. When his various wives came to Jerusalem to take up residence there, they brought their favourite idols with them and arrangements had to be made for their distinctive forms of worship. (11:6–13, 31–33). No longer could the people look up to the king as an inspiring spiritual example.

Solomon's desire to build a worthy temple was commendable, but he also initiated a series of other over-ambitious building projects (7:1–12) which could only be carried out with the aid of compulsory labour gangs (4:6; 5:13–18; 9:15). During four months of every year, thirty thousand Hebrew men would be away from their homes, wives and families. If this compulsory service had only been for a limited period, during the building of the temple, it would have been gladly undertaken by the majority. But the whole complex of extensive and elaborate buildings in Jerusalem almost dwarfed the actual temple. The House of the Forest of Lebanon, for example, (7:2–5) was far larger than the temple. Much of this enforced work was merely to satisfy Solomon's lust for opulence and fame.

Furthermore, these compulsory periods of service in Jerusalem were not merely a *personal* inconvenience for family men; they made for serious economic instability throughout the whole country. These four-month sessions robbed a man of any opportunity to earn money for the upkeep of his own family left back at home without father and bread-winner. Solomon certainly became wealthy, but at whose expense? The long-term effects of Solomon's unfortunate economic policy can be clearly seen in the sequence of seriously disruptive events which quickly followed his death. He may have been wise at the beginning of his reign, but he appears

to have lost all sense of spiritual priority before the end
of it.

2. A DIVIDED KINGDOM (1 Kings Chapter 12 to 2 Kings Chapter 17)

The story that follows is not a happy one. The acces-
sion of Solomon's son, Rehoboam, provided the opportunity for the revolt of the northern tribes led by Jeroboam. The people's objection to Solomon's irksome
policies can be seen in their strong request for their
burdens to be eased. The division of the kingdom might
well have been avoided if young Rehoboam had taken
the advice of the older men at his court. The fact that
the rebels stoned Solomon's leading taskmaster is
particularly significant (12:1–19). In order to unify the
northern tribes, Jeroboam introduced idolatrous worship
(12:20–33), and so began a long period of religious
apostasy and moral decline. The northern part of the
disrupted kingdom became known as *Israel*; the southern
part was called *Judah*. The capital of the north was later
established at Samaria, while Jerusalem obviously remained as the metropolis of the south.

The usual plan of the writer of this 'prophetic history'
is to outline the reign of a particular king and then relate
contemporary events in the opposite kingdom, though
there are occasional interruptions in a story to point
out important happenings in the neighbouring territory.
During part of the ensuing story the two nations became
pathetically involved in warfare against each other; this
was particularly so at the beginning of the divided kingdom's history. Judah's king, Rehoboam, and Israel's
Jeroboam (12:1–14:31) were often in conflict (15:6).
This sad state of affairs continued for some time and
was only brought to a close as the northern kingdom

became involved in serious internal strife and division. Abijam ruled over Judah for a brief period (15:1–8) and he was followed by Asa who was on the throne for over forty years (15:9–24). He tried to remove the idolatry in the land with its inevitable immoral associations.

Turning again to the north, we find that Jeroboam's son, Nadab, succeeded to the throne of Israel, but, after a brief reign of two years, he was killed by Baasha who also destroyed every other member of Jeroboam's family (15:33–16:7). Baasha was on the throne for twenty-four years and was succeeded by his son, Elah; his brief reign (16:8–14) was brought to an abrupt end by his military commander, Zimri, who murdered his king during a drunken orgy at Tirzah. Zimri only enjoyed the royal title for a week (16:15–20), at the end of which he committed suicide in his palace because Omri, a military leader, had been elected to kingship by the people (16:21–28). During this reign Samaria was built and became recognised as the capital of the north, but Omri was more corrupt and disobedient to God's Word than any of his predecessors since the time of Jeroboam (16:25–27). His son, Ahab, followed him (1 Kings 16:29–22:40) and at this point in the narrative the prophet Elijah emerges as a courageous, spiritual leader. Ahab also ignored God's warning regarding foreign wives and married Jezebel, the daughter of the king of Sidon. She was a devout Baal-worshipper and made the already poor spiritual condition of Israel far worse than it had ever been before.

Elijah is seen in these stories as a second Moses, a zealous champion for the Law of God. He was so deeply concerned about the nation's apostasy that he pleaded with God that a famine might come (17:1; Jas. 5:17), even though he might well have died in it. Moses was willing to be blotted out of the book (Exod. 32:32) if only his people might be spared, and Elijah had similar heroism. God not only provided for his material needs during the long famine (17:1–16); He also protected the prophet from Ahab's many spies and soldiers (18:10). Elijah was instructed by God to call the Baal-prophets to Mount Carmel for a public test as to the power of their deity. Baal was shown to be yet another worthless idol and Jehovah was revealed as the only true God (18:1–46). In her fury the queen ordered the execution of Elijah and this brave prophet became suddenly afraid and fled to Horeb for safety (19:1–8). God met him there, assured him that he was not Israel's only believer, and told him to anoint his successor, Elisha, a young farmer at Abel-meholah (19:9–21). War broke out between Israel and Syria during which time an alliance was made between Israel and Judah, the latter nation being at that time under the rule of Jehoshaphat, a godly king. In a combined encounter with the Syrian army, Ahab was killed (20:1–22:40). A brief account of the reigns of Jehoshaphat (Judah) and Ahaziah (Israel) brings the First Book of Kings to a close (22:41–53).

The downfall (literally!) of Ahaziah is told at the beginning of the Second Book of Kings (1:1–18) followed by a brilliant narrative which describes the miraculous departure of Elijah (2:1–12). At this point his prophetic successor, Elisha, begins to dominate the scene and his exploits occupy most of the early chapters of the book (2:13–8:15). They reveal him as a man of spiritual ambition (2:9–10), undaunted faith (2:13–14), immense courage (3:13–14), evident holiness (4:9), believing prayer (4:32–37), astonishing perception (6:8–19; 6:32–7:2, 17–20; 8:1–2, 7–15) and rich compassion (6:20–23).

The compiler of this history then gives brief summaries of the reigns of Jehoram (8 : 16–24) and Ahaziah (8 : 25–29) of Judah, followed by a more detailed account of a revolution in the northern kingdom led by Jehu, a military captain who was secretly anointed as king on the specific instructions of Elisha. The kings of Israel (Joram) and Judah (Ahaziah), at this time related by marriage, were assassinated and in the ensuing revolution Jehu was used to remove all Baal worship from the land (9 : 1–10 : 36). After the death of Jehu, the story in the northern kingdom is an increasingly depressing one, and things were not much better in the south. A cruel queen (Athaliah) ruled over Judah for a few years (11 : 1–20) followed by Jehoash, or Joash (11 : 21–12 : 21). During his reign various repairs were undertaken to the Jerusalem Temple. Life in the northern kingdom became terribly corrupt again; Jehoahaz (13 : 1–9) and Jehoash (13 : 10–13, not to be confused with the king of Judah of the same name!) were both evil. After an account of the death of Elisha (13 : 14–25) the narrative then moves to southern kingdom affairs under the rule of Amaziah (14 : 1–22) during which period Israel and Judah were again in conflict. After this, Jeroboam II (Jeroboam ben Joash) became king in Israel and his reign was economically prosperous but religiously, morally and socially corrupt. It is important for us to observe at this point that Amos and Hosea exercised their rich prophetic ministry during this spiritually decadent period (14 : 23–29; Amos 1 : 1; Hos. 1 : 1). Azariah (also called Uzziah) then came to the throne of Judah (15 : 1–7); more detail is given of his reign in the second book of Chronicles. He is a vivid and tragic example of the man who begins well but ruins his God-given opportunity by becoming arrogant and self-confident (15 : 5; 2 Chron. 26 : 15–20).

Serious internal strife then characterised the life of
the northern kingdom, Israel. During this time a series
of different kings came to the throne, usually for brief
periods. Several of these kings were assassinated (15 : 8–
31). The structure of national life was beginning to
crumble in the north. As for Judah, things had improved
spiritually under Jotham (15 : 32–38), but idolatry and
unhelpful foreign alliances were later introduced by his
successor, Ahaz (16 : 1–20). Isaiah and Micah ministered
in Judah during this period, and also through the later,
and better, reign of Hezekiah. By this time the Assyrian
armies were threatening the peace of both north and
south. Israel formed an alliance with Syria and attempted resistance, but Ahaz of Judah preferred to
become a vassal state of Assyria. Hoshea became Israel's
last king. His capital city, Samaria, was beseiged by the
Assyrian troops for three dreadful years and finally sur-
rendered in 721 BC. With the collapse of the city came
the end of the northern kingdom. In this 'prophetic
history' it is clearly viewed as an act of divine judgment (17 : 1–23). It was the practice of these near-eastern
conquerors to carry away into captivity any members
of society who might later be instrumental in leading a
revolt against their oppressors. These leading citizens
were invariably replaced by people from the conquerors
own land. The intermarriage of these Assyrians with
Israelites led to the formation of a racial group which
later became known as the 'Samaritans' (17 : 24–41).
While spiritual things declined in the north, Isaiah and
Micah both preached in Judah about similar dangers
which would befall them if they did not turn to God in
penitence and trust.

3. A DECLINING KINGDOM (2 Kings Chapters 18–25)

From this point in the narrative, interest is focused entirely on the surviving kingdom of Judah. It is another sad story of serious spiritual decline, broken only by the good reigns of Hezekiah and Josiah, who both initiated reformations of immense religious importance, but of very limited duration. Throughout this closing period, Judah was a vassal state of Assyria, though the era did witness two or three quite active rebellions against the Assyrians. Hezekiah had the prophet Isaiah to support him at a time of national distress (18 : 1–20 : 21), but the king was followed on the throne by his utterly godless son, Manasseh. During Manasseh's reign the religious life of Judah became greatly depraved (21 : 1–18). Tradition has it that Isaiah was sawn in two at this time, although there is no biblical evidence to support this (21 : 16; 24 : 3–4; Heb. 11 : 37).

The brief reign of Manasseh's equally pagan son, Amon, was brought to a close by his assassination after he had been on the throne for only two years (21 : 19–26). His successor, Josiah, was made king at the early age of eight and his coronation marked the beginning of a period of spiritual improvement leading eventually to another reformation in Judah (22 : 1–23 : 30). During an extensive redecoration and repair programme to the Jerusalem temple a copy of 'the book of the law' was found (22 : 8–13) and this book was immediately made the basis of a radical reformation. It is more than likely that this discovery was either our present *Deuteronomy* or a major part of it. Josiah's reign came to an end when he became involved in warfare with Egypt and, during a fierce battle at Megiddo, was killed (23 : 28–30). The next two decades marked the end of the southern king-dom. In just over twenty years, four kings ruled over the depressed nation and their capital city was attacked and plundered on three different occasions (23:31–25:30). This period witnessed a series of sad and bitter tragedies for the people of God but during these difficult years God had his witnesses; Jeremiah and Zephaniah were both used by God as heralds of the truth in a period of unbelief and adversity.

A number of vital spiritual lessons can be discerned in this prophetic history recorded in the *First and Second Books of Kings*. There are four principles which appear quite frequently throughout these two books and are illustrated in the stories of Solomon, Jeroboam, Elijah and Jehoshaphat.

(i) *Selfish ambition affects others*

From the disappointing story of Solomon onwards, this danger is frequently expounded. Several kings failed because they acted solely on their own initiative and for their own materialistic advantage. Solomon started the unfortunate practice of strengthening economic security and political stability by the forming of an alliance with some heathen neighbour. With the alliance came the official treaty (to which we have already referred in our study of *Deuteronomy*); with the treaty came an agreement that homage should be paid to the deities to which each nation owed an allegiance. Solomon made matters far worse by marrying ungodly princesses in order to increase his already acknowledged international fame, but though he may have enjoyed a certain amount of pleasure and prestige because of these marital and international agreements the ultimate effect on the nation was spiritually distressing, morally degrading and nationally divisive. We bring sadness to others when we insist on pleasing ourselves.

(ii) Godless behaviour corrupts others

If Solomon illustrates the first lesson, Jeroboam is perhaps the most stark example of the second. The historian frequently refers to the highly contagious effect of idolatry and immorality. An old and almost blind prophet told Jeroboam's wife that God would give Israel up because of her husband's sins 'which he sinned and which he made Israel to sin' (1 Kings 14:16; 15:26, 30, 34; 16:2, 3, 13, 26; 21:22 and 2 Kings 3:3; 10:31; 13:6, 11; 14:24; 15:9, 18, 24, 28; 21:11, 16). It is frequently stressed in these books that when a king sins, he leads his people sadly astray. The recorder of this period of Hebrew history is at pains to demonstrate the indisputable fact that poor standards, low morals and ungodly conduct have an adverse effect on those who are nearest to us. No man can live entirely to himself; he invariably corrupts someone else by his ungodly behaviour.

(iii) Courageous witness inspires others

The depressing account of godless reigns is relieved here and there by the mention of some outstanding spiritual leader, usually a prophet, though occasionally a priest, who has the courage to speak out against the spiritual decadence of the nation. Elijah is perhaps the finest example of this kind of leader, but he is certainly not a solitary example. His fearless stand against four hundred Baal prophets on Mount Carmel is a vivid illustration of the immense spiritual confidence and fortitude of these heroic men. Elijah's bravery at this time was used to turn the tide spiritu-

F

ally. Every Christian's personal witness can be used to encourage his fellow believers to be more outspoken about their faith. Our cowardice may also be used by the devil to keep other believers' lips sealed.

(iv) *Personal holiness enriches others*

We have already observed that godless behaviour degrades other people; we must also recognise that the reverse is also true. If we live in a manner that glorifies God, other people will be definitely helped. The deeply committed, obedient Christian exercises a far greater influence over the lives of other people than he can ever fully know. Let our final illustration come from the life of a devout king of Judah, Jehoshaphat. At one period in his reign he endeavoured to help the king of Israel, at that time oppressed by the Moabites. Before they went to battle, Jehoshaphat asked for godly counsel from a prophet, and Elisha was invited to speak. The prophet made it clear to Jehoram, king of Israel, that he was intervening not because of his sake but because of the presence of a sincere and upright believer such as Jehoshaphat. The prophet's words are a constant reminder of the principle that personal holiness is honoured by God and used to the blessing of other people. Elisha turned to the unspiritual king Jehoram and said: 'As the Lord of hosts lives, whom I serve, were it not that I have regard for Jehoshaphat the king of Judah, I would neither look at you, nor see you' (2 Kings 3:14). The miraculous victory which followed was due solely to God's determination to acknowledge and reward the sanctity of his servant and, through his rich, personal devotion and commitment, bring deliverance to many others.

A Priest Looks at the Throne

THE *First and Second Book of Kings* present an account of Hebrew history from a distinctly *prophetic* point of view. The next group of twin-volumes goes by the un-usual name of *Chronicles*. Here again are two books, originally one in the Hebrew Bible, which also give an account of the history of the Jewish nation. But this time the story is viewed from the standpoint of a *priest*. Obviously there will be little point in covering the entire story again, but we must devote some time to the study of this fascinating twin-volume which, incidentally, is followed in our Bibles by *Ezra* and *Nehemiah*, another composite work, by either the same author or group of authors. There can be no doubt that *Chronicles–Ezra–Nehemiah*, as we know them, were compiled in the latter part of the Old Testament period, when the Jewish community had settled back in Jerusalem with the exile-experience well behind them. During the time they were in Babylon many of these exiles became interested in history with its many lessons from the past. Some wanted to account for their independent existence as a nation, so *Chronicles* was written.

Every historian writes from some particular point of view. Each '*fact*' that he presents is '*a selected fact*'; he does not include a mention of every single event in the history he is writing. When we come to study this priestly history, we must ask ourselves a question : why are certain important national issues left on one side, while others are more fully discussed with considerable attention to minute detail? Once we get a likely answer to that kind of question, we shall see that this 'history' is written for a specific teaching purpose. The selected facts become 'interpreted facts'. It is the religious life of God's people which interests him most. We do not know the name of the author of this group of writings (Chronicles–Ezra–Nehemiah) so we shall refer to him as 'the Chronicler'. We must try to get into his mind and to look carefully at the things which were of the greatest importance to him. In this way we may become better equipped to discern his spiritual message and to appreciate the inspiring books which, under the guidance of God's Spirit (2 Pet. 1 : 21) he wrote for our learning as well as for his contemporaries.

The exile-experience in Babylon may well have increased the interest of Jewish people in their history. The Jewish exiles constantly longed for home (Psa. 137 : 1–6) and, just as a modern immigrant loves to read about his home-country, so the Hebrew people became fascinated by the story of their interesting past. They wanted to know how they came into being, how God had led them through some difficult centuries, how they came to receive and at times reject their precious Law, why their king must be of the line of David, what the original temple was really like; these, and a host of other questions, crowded into the mind of many a Jewish believer. The literary work of the Chronicler is an answer to some of these questions. He used many different sources for his history and actually refers by name to about twenty of them (1 Chron. 5 : 17; 9 : 1; 23 : 27, etc.).

The two books we are now considering can be divided into four sections :

1. THEIR IMPRESSIVE ANCESTRY (1 Chronicles Chapters 1-10)

The first nine chapters contain long lists of genea-
logical tables, or 'family-trees'. What is of particular
interest for us is that in these lists the Chronicler almost
completely disregards the northern tribes. The break-
away of the northerners under Jeroboam I was regarded
as an act of serious apostasy and rebellion. God's purpose was that all the tribes should be united, living in
constant peace and giving each other mutual support.
When Jeroboam formed a separate kingdom (Israel) the
unity of the nation was shattered and life in the north
became degraded both religiously and morally.

Even in the presentation of these opening lists of
names the Chronicler compels us to listen to his important teaching. Three of his favourite themes are introduced in the first ten chapters, even though they are
not presented in any developed form. Bearing in mind
that the Chronicler is primarily concerned about the
spiritual life of the nation, we note here that he has
something to say in these opening chapters about God's
Word (obedience to God), prayer (approach to God) and
service (work for God); three themes of immense importance to the priesthood.

The first of these is presented negatively. Two
characters are introduced in this opening section of the
book, both of whom knew the word of God (the Law)
but did not obey it — Achan (2:7) and Saul (10:1-14).
Achan knew that all the spoil had to be 'devoted' to the
Lord (Joshua 6:17-19; 7:15-25) but he did not choose
to obey God's word. The Chronicler believed that,
similarly, King Saul 'died for his unfaithfulness' because
'he did not keep the command of the Lord' (10:13). The

second theme, that of prayer, introduces us to Jabez (4:9–10) and later to a large company of unnamed warriors from the tribes of Reuben, Gad and Manasseh (5:18–20). Jabez prayed with earnestness for God's bountiful provision and protection; the soldiers in the following chapter prayed for God's merciful intervention in a time of warfare. Both Jabez, the solitary man in need, and then the vast crowd of unnamed soldiers received divine help because they 'cried to God'. Service is the third topic. Details are given about the Levites and their appointment 'for *all* the service of the tabernacle of the house of God' (6:48), and some priests are later described as 'very able men for the work of the service of the house of God' (9:13). The first of these two references emphasises the fact that *all* the service for the tabernacle was effectively undertaken by this willing tribe (cf. 2 Chron. 30:22), the second stresses the immense variety of different gifts which were given to the service of God by those 'very able men' (cf. 1 Chron. 28:21). It was the Chronicler's skilful way of underlining the truth that only the best is good enough for God (2 Chron. 31:21).

2. THEIR IDEAL KING (1 Chronicles Chapters 11–21)

In the Chronicler's view Saul is a disobedient, self-centred transgressor, totally unsuitable for kingship. Therefore, this priestly historian is not in the least bit interested in his reign, even though there were some good things about it. As far as he is concerned, the only interest is that of pointing out the judgment of God on Saul's life: 'therefore the Lord slew him and turned the kingdom over to David, the son of Jesse' (10:14). With that stark comment a new section opens and its theme is that of the ideal king, David. The Chronicler is passionately interested in the great theme of the Davidic throne and there now follows a summary of the reign of David in eleven chapters, though we shall see as we read the chapters that this is selected history and what we have described as 'interpreted history'. David's family matters are usually left out of the story. No mention is made of his sin against Bathsheba and her husband Uriah. We read nothing about Absolom's sin of rebellion against his father. The Chronicler knows that he is not presenting us with a complete history of the Hebrew nation under David's rule. He is using selected narratives to emphasise certain spiritual truths; anything which does not serve his immediate purpose is left on one side. It can be read elsewhere. His themes in the David narrative are (i) *David's Colleagues* (11 : 1– 12 : 40): teamwork is a highly important subject in the Chronicler's approach to history (e.g. 1 Chron. 9 : 17–34; 15 : 16–24; 18 : 14–17; 28 : 21). (ii) *David's Devotion* (13 : 1–17 : 27). The story of the ark is told and the Chronicler is at pains to stress the importance of obedience to the law of God. The *Levites* carry the ark after the unhappy incident when it swayed and tottered on the cart (15 : 12–15, 26, 27). David is further portrayed as a submissive and dependent man who sought guidance from God in time of need (14 : 10, contrast 10 : 13– 14), and as one with a keen sense of spiritual priorities who longed to build a permanent home for the Ark of the Covenant (17 : 1–27). The King's passionate and practical concern about spiritual things was obviously of immense interest to a priestly writer. (iii) *David's Victories* (18 : 1–21 : 30). Clearly the Chronicler's inference here is that if you honour God, He will prosper you.

3. THEIR MAGNIFICENT SANCTUARY (1 Chronicles Chapter 22 to 2 Chronicles Chapter 9)

David's throne and Solomon's temple are the main themes of the Chronicler's work. These chapters deal with the temple, its administration, construction and dedication. Other details are given about Solomon's reign though, once again, the Chronicler is selective; nothing is said about Solomon's idolatry and his ungodly marriage alliances. 'Mixed marriages' were anathema to the Chronicler (see *Ezra–Nehemiah*) so he did not mention these failures in his account of Solomon's life and work.

4. THEIR CHEQUERED HISTORY (2 Chronicles Chapters 10–36)

Here again we are reading carefully selected extracts from Hebrew history. The Chronicler is not in the least bit interested in the northern kingdom (Israel) and he makes no direct mention of Israel unless it is in connection with an issue which directly affects the story of the south (Judah). One passage in this final section of the book which expounds the Chronicler's main interests is that which contains King Abijah's address to his northern kingdom opponents. In *1 Kings* Abijah (there called Abijam) is only known for his wickedness and wars (1 Kings 15:1–8) though reference is made to other details which can be read in 'the book of the Chronicles of the king of Judah' (1 Kings 15:7) obviously one of the sources used by the Chronicler. In *2 Chronicles* (13:4–12) King Abijah speaks to a vast array of Israelite soldiers and the issues which emerge in his address reflect many of the Chronicler's main interests – the united monarchy under David and his divinely ordained successors (13:4–7), the sin of idolatry (13:8), the divinely appointed priesthood and their helpers (13:9–10) and their insistence on correct sacrificial procedure in its proper setting, the Jerusalem temple (13:11–12).

Sins against the priesthood and all it stands for are naturally regarded as most serious. Saul sought guidance from a wizard rather than a priest or prophet (1 Chron. 10:13–14); Uzziah took priestly responsibilities upon himself and was punished by God for his pride (2 Chron. 26:16–21). The reverse is also true; those who put spiritual things first will be greatly helped and mightily blessed. Jehoshaphat is an outstanding example of this principle (2 Chron. 20:1–30).

It is in this fourth section that we can discern some of the great things which the Chronicler is wanting to say to us. We might summarise the main aspects of his teaching in this way:

(i) *Trust God*. The theme of absolute reliance upon the Lord is a highly important one in the Chronicler's thought (e.g. 2 Chron. 13:18; 14:11; 16:7–9; 20:5–17; 25:8; 32:7–8).

(ii) *Obey God*. The Law was obviously of immense interest to the Chronicler; those who obey God's word, and receive the advice of priests, will find themselves enriched and fortified (2 Chron. 14:2–4; 20:20; 23:18; 25:4; 30:16; 34:19–21, 31). Those kings who put away idolatry and other forms of corrupt worship are singled out for special commendation (2 Chron. 14:3–5; 15:8, 16; 17:6; 23:17; 31:1; 33:15; 34:3–7). Obversely, those who encourage false worship will be judged and punished (25:20).

(iii) *Honour God*. This priestly historian says in effect, 'Remember who God is, and adore Him. When God is honoured as God in our lives, there is no place for arrogant self-reliance.' Pride and self-sufficiency are regarded by him as among the worst sins. The Chronicler frequently calls his readers to humility and utter reliance on God.

(iv) *Seek God*. As a priest, this writer has an obvious interest in prayer. Those who seek God are helped; those who do not are chastised for their arrogant self-confidence (2 Chron. 14:7; 15:4, 12; 16:12; 17:3–4; 18:31; 20:3–4; 26:5; 30:18–19; 31:21).

Men with Difficult Tasks

In our previous study (*1 and 2 Chronicles*) we observed that the Books of *Chronicles*, *Ezra* and *Nehemiah* form a literary unity. They obviously belong to the same group of writings in the Old Testament and view Hebrew history from the same point of view. *Ezra* begins with a similar statement as that with which *2 Chronicles* ends (cf. Ezra 1:1–4 with 2 Chron. 36:22–23). It reminds us that when Cyrus, a previously insignificant tribal leader, conquered Babylon he allowed the Jewish exiles to return home to their own country. It cannot be said that vast numbers took advantage of his offer, for a majority had settled down comfortably in their new country and we know from archaeological discoveries that some of them had done reasonably well in business. They did not wish to face the upheaval of moving from one country to another. The *Book of Ezra* tells the story of two different contingents of Hebrews who ventured to make that long and dangerous journey home – the first company under the leadership of Sheshbazzar and Zerubbabel (Chapters 1–6) and the second many years later, under Ezra (7–10). After numerous discouragements the first company rebuilt the temple in Jerusalem encouraged in their work by the preaching of two prophets, Haggai and Zechariah. Under Ezra's leadership the second company concentrated their interest on the important work of spiritual reformation and renewal. The book can be simply divided into two main sections. Although its title is that of the dominant character in the book, Ezra himself does not appear until well into its second half.

1. BUILDING THE TEMPLE (Chapters 1–6)

It is extremely difficult to give precise dates to some of the events recorded in *Ezra* and *Nehemiah* and we content ourselves here with a simple suggestion as to the order of events in *Ezra–Nehemiah* which does not pretend to answer all the difficulties. Those who wish to study the history further should look at a more detailed book (e.g. *The New Bible Commentary Revised*, London, 1970, p. 395 ff or F. F. Bruce, *Israel and the Nations*, London 1969, p. 97–111). For our purposes we note that the first contingent of returned exiles was led by Shesh-bazzar (who seems to have been a younger son of King Jehoiachin) and Zerubbabel. These men had the respon-sibility of leading the exiled people home to Jerusalem and were encouraged to take back with them the valuable treasures which Nebuchadnezzar had removed from the Jerusalem temple many years before (1 : 1–4). Sheshbazzar seems to have had special responsibility for the valuables (1 : 5–11) and Zerubbabel may have had charge of the people themselves (2 : 1–70).

Once they arrived back in Judaea they gave imme-diate expression to their gratitude to God by celebrating the Feast of Tabernacles (3 : 1–5). This festival had been instituted many centuries before to remind the Hebrew people of their long journey through the wilderness from Egypt to the Promised Land (Lev. 23 : 34–43). Now these returned exiles had special cause for renewed thanksgiving; God in His mercy had brought them over seven hundred miles across another difficult wilder-ness, and they too wanted to acknowledge His goodness by holding this very significant feast. Do we express our gratitude to God for the way He has helped us day by day? The newly-settled people then started work on the rebuilding of the temple. This seemed to them an obvious spiritual priority (3:6–13), but all sorts of difficulties lay ahead. Some of their neighbours wanted to help but the returned exiles felt persuaded that it was best to carry through the work themselves. Many of those who had remained in the land had not kept absolutely true to the faith they once treasured and the newly settled citizens wanted to do it all for God out of a pure and sincere heart. Their opponents made mischief with the Persian authorities and one trouble followed another (4:1–24). Inevitably the work was held up for some time until a new king came to the Persian throne. The Jewish people were then given permission to continue, and eventually the work was finished. These chapters remind us of three great principles about our work for God:

(i) *God's work demands purity*

We may be tempted to think that the returned exiles were a little churlish to refuse the help of their neighbours and the people from the north (Samaritans). After all, we might argue, the more the merrier! But they knew that the worship of God had become corrupt and degraded and that many of these volunteers had mixed other religious notions and practices with their originally pure faith. We know that the people of the north were never popular with the Chronicler and, in any case, the ideals which prompted the refusal by the returned exiles were certainly exemplary. They were saying in effect, 'Only the best is good enough for God.' We may sometimes wonder whether they were being a bit priggish, but if we consider the unfolding story it can hardly be doubted that they were proved right in the end.

(ii) *God's work provokes opposition*

One reason we know that the returned exiles were wise in their refusal of assistance from Samaritans and others is that if their neighbours had been utterly sincere in their desire to help, they would hardly have turned so nasty when their offer was refused. If they had only desired to see a new temple built in Jerusalem, they would hardly have spent their time putting endless obstacles in the way of the builders. It is strange in a way, but God's work *always* meets with some kind of opposition. The devil does his best to raise difficulties and stir up enemies. If we find ourselves relatively free from this kind of attack from the devil, perhaps we ought to ask ourselves whether we are sufficiently active in vital Christian work (cf. 2 Tim. 3:12). After all, the Enemy is not likely to trouble us if we are not damaging his cause!

(iii) *God's work creates happiness*

Although there was intense opposition to the work, we must not run away with the idea that the temple rebuilding programme was a miserable enterprise. Once the returned exiles got down to it, they found that there was immense joy in God's service. The chapters contain some choice references to sincere thanksgiving, deep joy and abounding gratitude (3:11-13; 6:22). Those who are ready to 'put themselves out' in the service of God will find that they are not only happily occupied but also amply rewarded and constantly upheld.

2. Purifying the People (Chapters 7–10)

The story now moves to an account of the second contingent of returned exiles, this time under the leadership of the one from whom this book takes its title, Ezra. The stories told in these chapters reveal several of Ezra's rich qualities.

(i) He was *a man of faith*. Given the opportunity of leading a fresh company of people back from exile, he refused the offer of a proper military escort (8:22, 31) because he believed that that would have been lack of confidence in the God who had clearly promised to protect them. One of his favourite expressions was about the good hand of his God upon him (7:28; 8:22, 31) and he wanted the pagan authorities to know that he had proved the protecting presence of God many times in his experience.

(ii) Ezra was also *a man of prayer*. Once he got his large company of returned exiles back to the city he was astonished at the poor spiritual standard of the Jerusalem citizens. Many of the people had married partners who did not share their Hebrew faith, and this was an act of deliberate disobedience to the revealed Word of God to His people (9:1–10:1, cf. Exod. 34:14–16). Although he had not personally sinned in that way, Ezra was grieved about the transgression of the Jerusalem people and gave himself to prayer and repentance on their behalf.

(iii) He was also *a man of courage*. Once he got up from his knees, he knew what had to be done. These unhealthy marriage bonds would have to be severed. It seems rather harsh to us but it had led to widespread idolatry and in some cases gross impurity. Ezra knew that unless the returned community completely obeyed the commandments of God, they would never be truly happy and, even more serious, would never be used by God to the blessing and enrichment of others. A practically minded man named Shechaniah urged Ezra to take immediate action (10:2–5), and he got on with his unpleasant task. How wonderful that there was a man like that at Ezra's side just when he needed the moral courage and spiritual resolve to take action. The sad situation was put right (10:6–44) and ultimately the community was purified. The biblical story of the ongoing work of God often reminds us that God is pleased to work through two people in united and dependent partnership. Think about it—Moses and Aaron, Joshua and Caleb, Ezra and Shecaniah, Peter and Andrew, James and John, Paul and Barnabas, Peter and Mark, and so we could go on.

We have said one or two important things about *service* in this brief study of the *Book of Ezra*. Perhaps some of the most important truths about it are expressed by the Chronicler: 'And you, Solomon my son, know the God of your father, and serve him with *a whole heart* and with *a willing mind*; for the Lord searches all hearts, and understands every plan and thought. If you seek him, he will be found by you; but if you forsake him, he will cast you off for ever. Take heed now, for *the Lord has chosen you* to build a house for the sanctuary; *be strong, and do it*,' (1 Chron. 28:9–10).

Palace Steward becomes Successful Building Convener

THE next book in this Bible-library tells the exciting story of how the walls of Jerusalem were re-built under the leadership of Nehemiah, a 'cup-bearer' or steward at the palace of the Persian king. Walls were an absolute necessity for every Jewish city. Without them the communities were exposed to constant attack from neighbouring tribes. When King Nebuchadnezzar's soldiers took the leading Hebrew citizens into exile he made sure that the walls were broken down (2 Kings 25 : 10) so that the poor people who remained could not organise another revolt against him. As we have already seen, once the exile was over many Jews returned to their land and one of the most urgent tasks was the reconstruction of the walls and ruins so that the citizens could once again feel secure.

The story recorded in the *Book of Nehemiah* can be told under the following five headings:

1. PREPARATION (Chapters 1–2)

The story opens not in the depressed city of Jerusalem but in the Persian court where Nehemiah worked in a responsible position. Messengers from Judah informed Nehemiah of their trouble (1 : 1–3) and this sensitive man, eager to help his fellow believers, immediately prayed to God asking for His merciful forgiveness of the

nation's sins (1 : 4–7) and pleading that God would come
to the aid of His needy people (1 : 8–11). A man who
commits his cause so completely to God is sure to be
helped, and so the king gave his trusted servant permission to return to Jerusalem to execute this work
(2 : 1–9). But God's work is rarely allowed to proceed
unhindered or undisturbed. Two tribal leaders, who
lived near to Jerusalem, were exceptionally angry when
they heard that a highly capable man like Nehemiah
had come to help the citizens (2 : 10). Nehemiah realised
that the assignment was a huge one so, aware of the
opposition, he explored the ruined walls at night-time
(2 : 11–20). The time he spent in exploration was all
worth while. That night journey was an essential prelude to a magnificent re-building operation. God's work
is more important than anything else and always de-
serves careful thought and planning. Do we spend time
in thought and prayer before we embark on our work
for God, or is it all done in a frightful hurry and at the
last minute?

2. CO-OPERATION (Chapter 3)

At first sight, this next chapter seems to be a seemingly endless list of names. It is far from being that. Look
at it and read it carefully. It tells us about the various
people who worked together in this enterprise. This list
also has some wonderful spiritual treasures. It reminds
us, for example, that it has never been easy to get
'nobles' to do humble work for God (3 : 5 cf. 1 Cor.
1 : 26); that it is a good thing to work for God near your
own house (3 : 10, 23, cf. Mark 5 : 19); that over the centuries women folk have worked valiantly for God when
many men have been either too lazy, too cowardly or
too busy to serve Him (3 : 12, cf. Phil. 4 : 3); that some

people do their own share and then are happy to do even more for God (3:27); that if God's work is worth doing it is worth doing really well (3:20, AV, 'Baruch ... *earnestly* repaired the other piece') and so you could go on. All the Bible is 'profitable' wrote the apostle Paul (2 Tim. 3:16) and even lists of names have their lessons for us today. This chapter records a courageous and sacrificial venture in dedicated team work.

3. RESOLUTION (Chapters 4–7)

We have already mentioned the inevitable opposition they encountered (2:10, 19–20), and once the work was commenced all manner of obstacles were put in the way of the builders. The next few chapters tell the story of their enemies' attempt to bring the building operations to an end. They tried mockery (4:1) and scorn (4:2–3) and, when they found that bitter words did not worry the builders, they gathered their soldiers and prepared to attack the city (4:7–23) but without effect. In addition, Nehemiah not only had to supervise the building work but he also had to settle a number of serious difficulties among his own people (5:1–19). Even when his work of reconstruction was over the enemy still did not leave him alone (6:1–19). But thanks to God's good hand upon them and the hard work of a united team, the walls were re-built. The devil is always active and planning new ways of attacking God's people as they try to serve Him and please Him (1 Pet. 5:8). Many might well have been tempted to give up when the opposition increased but God's children must have firm resolution and a steadfast faith (1 Pet. 5:9).

4. DEDICATION (Chapters 8–12)

A great festival was held to celebrate the occasion and it was thought fitting that the Feast of Tabernacles (or Booths) would be a suitable way of giving expression to their gratitude to God. This feast recalled the long journey of the children of Israel through the wilderness, when they lived in booths or simple shacks (8:1–18). God's Word was read and the story of His generous and undeserved faithfulness was recalled (9:1–15). So also was the sad story of the ingratitude, rebellion and self-reliance of God's children (9:16–38). The people who were present at the festival once again affirmed their deep love for God and details are given of the joyful celebrations as they dedicated themselves afresh to Him (10:1–12:47).

5. REFORMATION (Chapter 13)

Nehemiah later returned to the Persian palace (13:6) but the king gave him permission to go back to Jerusalem. The leader knew that there were a number of things being tolerated by the people which were an offence to God. His Word (about mixed marriages, for example) was not obeyed, His house was not clean and His day was not honoured. Nehemiah's second visit to Jerusalem was not as a builder but as a reformer. To take one example, the Temple had become cluttered up with the goods and belongings of a completely pagan man who had formerly opposed God's work (13:4–8). It all had to be cleansed and thoroughly purified before it could be used for spiritually acceptable worship. Our lives sometimes get cluttered up with sad and sordid things and 'as temples of the Holy Spirit' (1 Cor. 6:19) these bodies of ours should be clean and pure.

The Book of Nehemiah urges us to do God's work thoroughly, to serve happily alongside other Christians, to be strong and resolute when opposition comes, to surrender ourselves to Him in loving obedience and constantly to keep our lives clean for His use.

God's Timing is Perfect

WE now come to *Esther*, a book which makes no mention whatever of God's Name, though His work is evident in every chapter. It tells the story of a new queen who was chosen to sit alongside the king of Persia. Her name was Esther and she was a Jewess. Her relation and guardian, Mordecai, had taught her the Jewish faith and once she was crowned queen the Jews began to see that this regal appointment was really a *divine* appointment. At that very time the Jewish people were subject to sinister opposition from enemies at court and throughout the entire kingdom they were under the threat of imminent death. As this unjust sentence hung like a heavy cloud over every Jewish home, the young queen Esther went into the presence of the king to acquaint him with the plight of her people. The book tells of the deliverance of the Jewish people and of the judgment of God upon Haman, the influential courtier who had plotted for their extermination.

What is this little book saying to us about our lives today? It simply underlines two great biblical truths:

1. GOD'S CONTROL OVER NATIONS

The historical setting of this dramatic story is important. You will remember that we have earlier seen that when King Cyrus of Persia conquered the Babylonian nation he allowed the Jewish exiles to return home to Judaea. Some of them did not make that journey and chose to remain behind in that alien land. The story found in *Esther* records something of their tribulation. Haman hated the Jewish people and wanted to get rid of them (3 : 5 f). But the welfare of the Jews was not in the hands of Haman or the Persian king but in the hands of God. The main message of the book is that God rules over the world and His purposes for His people cannot be frustrated by mere men. Proverbs 21 : 1 is an interesting brief commentary on this story : 'The king's heart is a stream of water in the hand of the Lord; He turns it wherever He will.'

2. GOD'S CONCERN FOR INDIVIDUALS

He not only rules over the nations as Sovereign, but plans for individual lives as a Father. Every one is dear to Him, and He makes constant provision for their care. The story in this book focuses on His Fatherly care over two individuals in particular, Esther and her guardian, Mordecai. The Lord God knew that His people's lives would be in peril so He planned that young Esther should be chosen as the next queen. This young woman had to make the needs of her people known to the king and this meant going into the audience chamber uninvited (5 : 1 f). But although this was a breach of court-etiquette at that time, she took the risk even though the king's disapproval would have led to her death. God saw to it that she was protected and her courageous action was rewarded. Mordecai believed that Esther had been put into that privileged place of access at the Persian court by the God who carefully plans the lives of His children. He expressed the truth of this in memorable words : 'And who knows whether you have not come to the kingdom for such a time as this?' (4 : 14).

God was not only planning in Esther's life, however.

He was at work in the circumstances of her guardian's life also. Mordecai had earlier discovered the secret details of a grim plot against the life of the Persian king (2:21–23). The details of this attempted assassination had been carefully recorded in the royal archives but had not been brought to the attention of the king. At the very time when the Jewish people were in danger, the king asked for the records to be read to him and he heard of Mordecai's fidelity and loyalty. As a result, Mordecai was suitably rewarded (6:1–12). Haman's subsequent actions resulted in his being executed on the very gallows he had built for Mordecai (7:10), and the Jewish people throughout the Persian empire were released from the awful threat of extermination.

The Jews were so relieved and grateful that they commemorated God's merciful deliverance in a special festival called Purim. They knew that God's providential care ought not to be forgotten and so each year they kept this feast and so recalled the story of Esther's courage, Mordecai's loyalty and, most of all, God's unchanging faithfulness and might. The tale ought to encourage us, especially during those times in all our lives when things seem to go wrong, when one grim difficulty or disaster follows hard upon another and we are tempted to think that God has abandoned us. In these moments we should remember the story of Esther and realise that the God who planned for her will never desert us either.

Even Suffering has its Value

FOR centuries men have talked about 'the patience of Job'. The book which bears his name tells the story of a prosperous and devout landowner and possibly belongs to the earliest period of biblical history. It relates the anguish and suffering which came into the life of one of the most godly men of his time and one of its aims is to show that, in our moments of adversity, we must not immediately jump to the conclusion that our physical suffering is God's way of inflicting punishment upon us. People are often tempted to think like this though they do not always phrase it in precisely that way. Usually they say something like 'I can't think what I've done to deserve this', but it means very much the same. It is all based on the age-old supposition that without exception righteous people must prosper and unrighteous people must eventually suffer. But the psalmist (see Psalms 37 and 73) proved that the reverse is often the case. Those who deliberately shut God out of their lives will ultimately have to face Him in judgment and, at the same time, those who are utterly dedicated to Him must remember that they do not thereby escape from trouble.

The Book of Job has a superbly written prologue (1:1–2:13) and an equally magnificent epilogue (42: 1–17). Between these opening and closing chapters a series of conversations are recorded which took place between Job and his friends (Chapters 3–37). These speeches form the main part of the book and they are recorded in detail so that we can all understand something of Job's increasing anguish and also how easy it is for well-meaning people to misunderstand God's sovereign purposes for men.

The three friends who first emerge are called Eliphaz, Bildad and Zophar. They have a lot to say and they look at Job's problem from different points of view but all three are agreed that he must have been an awful sinner to have become such a pitiful sufferer (Chapters 4–31). They are utterly ignorant of what has gone on in the heavenly court (1:6–12; 2:1–6). They do not realise that Job is a 'test-case' for righteousness, nor how deeply God loves him. All their comments are from the point of view of a man of this world, obviously religious but sadly misguided. At the end of this drama, God's word of condemnation thunders out, and all those who speak carelessly or hastily about the problem of suffering must remember it: 'You have not spoken of me what is right' (42:7–8). These men were undoubtedly sincere, unquestionably devout and firmly convinced— but they were terribly wrong in their judgments.

A younger man than the other three, Elihu, is the next friend who comes to help Job and offer some kind of consolation (Chapters 32–37). He is not so hasty in his condemnation and he comes somewhere near to a solution. Elihu believes that suffering has educative value. Man can learn from it. At times young Elihu sounds a bit arrogant but he has some extremely helpful things to say. In superb language he reminds us of our limited knowledge: 'Do you know the balancings of the clouds, the wondrous works of Him who is perfect in knowledge?' (37:16).

These observations by Elihu prepare the way for one

of the most majestic passages in the whole Bible. God speaks and reminds Job of His majesty and wisdom as the Almighty Creator (Chapters 38–41). It is done in the form of a series of massive questions which God hurls one after the other at the bewildered and resentful Job. This humiliating encounter brought Job to his knees in humble submission (42 : 1–17). He confessed that this last experience in which he had almost seen God face to face and through which he had certainly been made aware of His greatness and glory, had enabled him to realise his mistake in trying to justify himself before man. God's will, he acknowledged, was best for his life even though he did not fully understand God's dealings with him.

What is this wonderful book saying to us in our day? It says:

1. ACKNOWLEDGE YOUR LIMITATIONS

We do not know everything. If Job had only known, when his calamities and adversities came, all that we know about God's concern for him and God's pleasure in him (1 : 8; 2 : 3) he would not have spoken carelessly and angrily about the God who loved him so deeply. The great speeches of the Creator-God (Chapters 38–41) are designed to impress upon us, as well as this righteous sufferer, the limitations of our knowledge. In our moments of agony and grief we must believe that the One who knows all, orders the best for His children.

2. GUARD YOUR SPEECH

The main lesson to be learnt from Job's friends is that, however convinced we may be, we should be extremely careful about what we say to people in serious trouble. Kind words can be used to heal some grim wounds but thoughtless words can intensify grief and make a sufferer even more unhappy. When the friends first met Job they sat quiet for a week. When our own friends are in deep trouble our presence and companionship, our kind deeds, our strong and firm handshake, can often accomplish far more than a torrent of words.

3. Examine Your Heart

If you are in trouble yourself at this time, the *Book of Job* has many vital things to say to you. It urges you not to be resentful or bitter but to look deeply into your own needy heart and mind and ask God to use this trouble to bring you nearer to Him. Adversity can have a corrective ministry in our lives (Heb. 12 : 3–13). It can be used to make us more aware of our dependence upon God.

4. Consider Your Friends

The sad thing about Job's friends is that by their careless preaching they disappointed him so deeply (6 : 14 f). They appeared to him like a mountain stream which in the rainy season was full of sparkling water but once the rains stopped it was dry. He looked to them hoping to have his thirst quenched but was bitterly disappointed. One of the good things that comes out of trouble is that it helps us to be far more sensitive to the needs of others. The man or woman who has had an almost completely trouble-free life is rarely sought after by harassed souls. J. M. Barrie said that because his mother had lost a baby, other distressed mothers would turn to her in the hour of their anguish.

5. RELINQUISH YOUR RESENTMENTS

Job had every reason to be miserable at the reactions of his useless friends. They seemed to make his trouble worse instead of better but the epilogue of the book tells us that Job was brought to the place where, instead of fighting them, he prayed for them. 'And the Lord turned the captivity of Job when he prayed for his friends' (42 : 10, AV). It is an exultant climax to an otherwise bitter episode. In those moments of prayer he anticipated the words of the Lord Jesus, who surely knew what suffering was. 'Pray for those who abuse you . . . forgive and you will be forgiven' (Luke 6 : 28, 37).

6. TRUST YOUR CREATOR

The main message of this *Book of Job* is that we must learn to trust the God who made us, even though at times we are bewildered and baffled by the adverse circumstances of our lives. He reigns and all that has happened has not escaped His notice. Always remember that as our loving Father He cannot allow His children to be tested beyond their capacity to endure (1 Cor. 10 : 13).

The Finest Hymn Book in the World

It seems as though God's people have been singing from the beginning of time. They have sung in joy (Exod. 15:1–21) and also in sorrow (2 Sam. 1:17–27). Many of the great songs of Old Testament times were composed by a small group of people and among the leading writers of these spiritual songs King David has a prominent place. These songs are collected in one book though several other 'psalms', as we call them, are found in other parts of the Bible.

The Book of Psalms presents us with a superb collection of 150 hymns of various kinds. Some have exultant themes of joy and gratitude, others sound the deep and sombre notes of depression, guilt and despair. Martin Luther called them 'Little Bibles' in that they reflect some of the great themes of Scripture and often lead us from the place of grim despondency to jubilant thanksgiving.

Obviously we cannot possibly comment on all the psalms and, in a sense, they do not need the kind of introduction which is helpful if not essential in the case of many other Old Testament books. The hymn-book of the Old Testament accurately reflects our varying spiritual conditions and all of us have been helped on many different occasions by a favourite psalm. There have also been times when an unfamiliar psalm has been used by God to bring us to the place of pardon or peace, security and trust. Wavering faith has been firmly established and deep darkness has been turned to light as we have turned the pages of this indescribably beautiful hymnal.

In a time of temptation Psalm 1 has brought help to millions. In a time of sleeplessness God's people have been helped by Psalm 4. People who have suffered because of the slanderous accusations of their enemies have realised that David went through their agony of mind and spirit and Psalm 7 has brought them immense comfort as well as necessary warning. A profound sense of gratitude for all the wonders of the created world has struck men afresh as they have read Psalms 8, 19, and 66.

Over the centuries the desolate experience of suffering and anguish has been made bearable in the lives of many believers by reading Psalm 22. They have realised that these words were on the lips of their Lord as He died for them on the Cross and they too have been brought to the place of submission and trust. What immeasurably rich help Christian people have received from the Shepherd Psalm (23). When surrounded by enemies, daunted by opposition, or haunted by fears, Psalms like 27, 28, 31, 35, 37, 40, 43, 44, 46, 57, 61, 62, 63, 68, 71, 91 (and a host of others) have brought strength and peace. In those dark moments of grief and remorse for our sin and stupidity we, like millions of others, have found that a psalm has met our need and brought us to the place of confession, penitence and ultimate peace. Look at them again if this describes your condition (Psalms 32, 51).

Many of these psalms have provided us with words of profound gratitude and sincere worship. A. J. Gossip used to describe adoration as 'thinking magnificently about God' and Psalms like 95, 96, 97, 145 to 150 have helped to do just that. Some of these glorious songs have inspired us (103, 104, 107, 115), others have rebuked us (139) but, at some time or other, most of them have helped us. Their acute sense of history has frequently reminded us of the comforting and sustaining truth that God has never forsaken His people (44, 80, 89, 90). The longest Psalm (119) has renewed our confidence in God's own Word and its relevance at all times. What a treasure this hymn book is. Turn to it again. Let it encourage you to worship with your friends in God's house (Psa. 5, 84, 116, 134, 138) and let it be your companion in the secret place of daily prayer and private worship (Psa. 130, 142).

A book like Prothero's *Psalms in Human Life* (often found in second-hand bookshops) will convince you that millions before you have found refreshment and renewal in this amazing collection of beautiful hymns. It is for your help too.

This Way to Happiness

You may well be familiar with that wonderful passage from the teaching of Jesus which we sometimes call 'the Beatitudes' (Matt. 5:1–12). This name is given to these famous sayings because each one begins in an identical way—'*Blessed is* . . .' or '*Oh! the happiness* of the meek, pure in heart, poor in spirit . . .' The Old Testament also has its beatitudes. On many occasions in the Old Testament we read 'Blessed is the man . . .' It is found in the biblical book we have just considered and is given an important place in the opening verses of some familiar Psalms (e.g. 1, 32, 41, 119, 128). It also provides us with a clue to the meaning of the next book in our Bible-library—*Proverbs*. This very practical, down-to-earth book presents us with a series of extremely important lessons about everyday life. It points the way to happiness and perhaps we might use some of the beatitudes of *Proverbs* to direct us to the main lessons in this helpful book.

In deep concern for the spiritual welfare of His people God raised up several different kinds of leaders. We have already seen that the *priests* had an important function to perform though, as we shall see later, the role of the *prophets* became increasingly important as the years went by. Scribes or *wise men* formed a third group. They collected and recorded some of the wise-sayings of the past and have been called 'the interpreters of Hebrew religion'. They took some of the great eternal truths

H

which God had given to them and related them to every-day affairs in the home, family and wider community. *Proverbs* contains a vast number of such sayings and its beatitudes may lead us to some of the main aspects of its teaching.

The compiler of this collection of famous proverbs would say that the way to happiness is:

1. A WAY OF WISDOM

This is a key idea in the book. For the first beatitude look up Proverbs 3:13. 'Happy is the man who finds wisdom and the man who gets understanding.' It is the wise-man's way of saying that we cannot cope with the problems and difficulties of life by our own limited intelligence. We need wisdom, a deep spiritual insight which God promises to give to those who seek it, and to those who acknowledge their need of His help in life (Jas. 1:5). This teaching about 'seeking wisdom' is found again and again in *Proverbs* (e.g. 1:1–6, 2:6–15) and it should remind us of our need of God's guidance every day of our lives.

2. A WAY OF OBEDIENCE

Yet, wisdom itself is not enough. What is the use of knowing what is the really wise thing to do in any situation if, in point of fact, you do not do it? The next beatitude in *Proverbs* (8:32) stresses the necessity of obeying God. 'Happy are those who keep my ways.' Once we know exactly what He wants us to do we must bring our immediate obedience to Him. Never forget the words of Mary, the mother of Jesus: 'Do whatever He tells you' (John 2:5).

3. A WAY OF DISCIPLINE

But somebody may well ask, 'How can I know what God wants me to do?' Turn to the next beatitude (Prov. 8:34) and see that listening to God must be a daily discipline. We must set aside some time in each day to hear what He is saying to us through His Word, the Bible. 'Happy is the man who listens to me watching *daily* at my gates, waiting beside my doors.' The doors and gates were the places where the servants stood waiting attentively for the Master's voice. It must be a *daily* habit. Set aside some time in each day, preferably in the morning, when God can speak to you through this marvellous Book, the Bible. This 'Quiet Time', as we sometimes call it, is an indispensable part of every Christian's life.

4. A WAY OF LOVE

We have already seen that *Proverbs* is an intensely practical book. It will not allow us to become pre-occupied with our own interests. It says 'What about the needs of others?' God is not only concerned about us as individuals but about all people, and He wants to use us to bring help to others. Here is the next beatitude in the book (14:21): 'He who despises his neighbour is a sinner, but happy is he who is kind to the poor.' The compiler of *Proverbs* has a fear of empty speech and mere words. He knows that people in distress, poverty or want of any kind need acts of love and kindness. A careful reading of the book will suggest several ways by which we can help our neighbours and friends. Jesus told his disciples that these acts of generous love could be used to bring people to God (Matt. 5:16). This theme of kindness and consideration is often expounded in

Proverbs in practical terms. If you want to be kind to your neighbour *do not gossip* (11:13; 15:1-4; 25:9-11). If you want to prepare for the future, *do not be idle* (6:6-11). If you want to be useful in the community, *do not be greedy* (11:24-25). There are many other examples in the book of this practical emphasis.

5. A WAY OF TRUST

'Happy is He who trusts in the Lord' (16:20); this is the next beatitude. The wise-men realised that those who want to live for God will often find themselves up against difficulties of various kinds and they often urged the people to put their trust in God. Proverbs 3:5-6 is one of the really well-known sayings of the book and it focuses on the need for complete trust in the God who will never let us down: 'Trust in the Lord with all your heart, and do not rely on your own insight. In all your ways acknowledge Him and He will make straight your paths.' Look up 11:28; 28:26 to see how the wise-men developed this theme of trust and warned the people about putting their trust or confidence in the wrong things.

6. A WAY OF WORSHIP

One word which constantly recurs in *Proverbs* is 'fear' and this leads us to our next beatitude: 'Blessed is the man who fears the Lord always' (28:14). When the Bible says we have to fear God it does not mean we must be frightened of Him. It means we are to put Him first. We are to honour Him and worship Him as God. As Martin Luther put it we are to 'let God be God', that is we must constantly acknowledge His supreme control over every part of our lives.

A Gloomy Man Speaks Out

NOBODY would pretend that the message of the book called *Ecclesiastes* is easy to understand. Like *Proverbs* it belongs to a type of biblical writing which we call 'Wisdom Literature'. Here again we find a collection of pithy sayings about life but the author and compiler of *Ecclesiastes* is temperamentally quite different from the wise-men whose sayings are found in *Proverbs*. A bright radiance pervades the book of *Proverbs* even though at times the teaching touches on some very serious themes. *Ecclesiastes* on the other hand tends to have a rather heavy and gloomy aspect. What is it all about?

It is likely that the Holy Spirit allowed the *Book of Ecclesiastes* to be written so that we might be able to see how a man looks at life and its problems from a purely human, this-world point of view. Such an outlook is bound to be depressing. It is inclined to ignore the great facts of God's sovereign control and providential care. It is the outlook of a man who has not fully discovered all the wonders of God's majesty and mercy. In some ways it is almost the viewpoint of the rich farmer in our Lord's parable (Luke 12 : 19): 'Eat, drink, be merry.' Two words which stick in our minds on reading through this book are *materialism* and *pessimism*.

Time and again the 'man' of Ecclesiastes invites us to enjoy ourselves to the full because there is nothing else to live for! Look at 8 : 15, for example. On several occasions the writer (or 'the Preacher' as he calls himself)

says that it is God's will that we should get the maxi-
mum amount of pleasure from life (2:24; 3:12–13;
5:19; 9:7). While it is true that, to use the apostle Paul's
words, He 'giveth us richly all things to enjoy' (1 Tim.
6:17, AV) there is more to life than an endless round of
pleasure-seeking. 'The Preacher' of Ecclesiastes makes no
secret of the fact that no amount of wealth or pleasure
gives a man abiding satisfaction (2:1–11; 6:2). In this
state of deep unhappiness nothing brings him joy, and
life appears to have no real meaning. In fact he says that
life and everything in it is 'vanity'—a word that really
means 'nothingness'. This grim despair confronts the
reader of the book time and again and even life after
death seems to have nothing to offer (3:18–4:3). It is
certainly the outlook of a man who lacks deep insight
into immense and thrilling truths of God's sovereign rule
and His providential care. There is more to life than
sighing! Yet *Ecclesiastes* is a most important book for
our own generation. Many people are searching for a
meaning and a purpose to our existence and in their
emptiness and sad yearning they long for some clue as
to the meaning of man's life on earth. This book exposes
the thinking of such a person and is of the utmost value
to us in our contemporary situation.

Lest it be thought that its only value is a negative one
(i.e. 'Don't let this happen to you!') it must be said that
'the Preacher' has many rich insights. Read the book
through again and make a note of some of the truths that
are of glorious importance to us all. He reminds us, for
example, that there is a right time for everything and
part of the art of living is that of choosing the right
moment (3:1–8). He says that hard work is one of God's
choice gifts to men. God is a Creator and Worker and
His plan is that man should work as well. People without

useful work are people without contentment, simply because God has made us that way (2:24; 3:13; 9:10). 'The Preacher' obviously values his friends for he has a lovely passage about the joys of companionship (4:9–12). He tells us how to go to God's house and warns us not to make rash vows which we have no intention of keeping (5:1–6). He reminds us that wisdom, the knowledge of how to do the right thing at the right time, is far better than strength and he tells a superb little story to illustrate it (9:13–17). He warns us about the dangers of putting things off when they ought to be done at once (11:4). He urges the youth of his day to remember the God who made him (12:1) and he tells us all, young and old alike, that the clue to life is to worship God and obey Him (12:13). These closing words are probably his best.

True Love and its Tests

No library would be complete without a love story and if that is the kind of story which you like to read, the Bible will not disappoint you. It has quite a few love stories but its longest is called *The Song of Solomon*. It tells the simple tale of a girl (called a Shulammite), who was in love with a young shepherd. It seems from the story that King Solomon also became attracted to her and the details of the story suggest that she spent some time at the royal palace. Her true lover searched for her and longed for her to return to their simple life in the country. Eventually she realised how deeply she loved him and responded to his persistent invitation to become his partner in life.

It is not wise to dogmatise about the precise details of the story and if you care to read it through for yourself it may well suggest other details, or even variants, to you. Why is it in the Old Testament? It is there surely because the Lord God is interested in *all* life and not just in what we might sometimes call 'spiritual life'. He does not make sharp distinctions between sacred and secular, as we do all too often. If we love Him, we shall hand our individual lives over to Him, believing that matters regarding relationships, friendships, love-affairs and choosing the right partner in life are of immense importance to the God who loves us utterly and completely. After all He loved us before anyone else loved us. Good parents are obviously concerned about their children's friendships. They long that their lives will be made more happy by their relationship with others. If human parents are so deeply concerned about such things how much more must God care about His children and their relationships. The Bible has a good deal to say about love, and this unique book, *The Song of Solomon*, has many choice things to share with us on this immense theme.

1. It illustrates in several places something of *the joy that love brings* (2:10–13). The person in love falls in love with everything else, and it is a beautiful parable of what happens when we come to love the Lord Jesus and receive Him as our own Saviour and Lord. D. L. Moody, the great evangelist of the nineteenth century, once put it like this:

'I remember the morning on which I came out of my room after I had first trusted Christ. I thought the old sun shone a good deal brighter than it ever had before—I thought that it was just smiling upon me; and as I walked out upon Boston Common and heard the birds singing in the trees, I thought they were all singing a song to me. Do you know, I fell in love with the birds. I had never cared for them before. It seemed to me that I was in love with all creation. I had not a bitter feeling against any man, and I was ready to take all men to my heart. If a man has not the love of God shed abroad in his heart, he has never been re-generated. If you hear a person get up in the prayer-meeting and he begins to find fault with everybody, you may doubt whether his is a genuine conversion; it may be counterfeit. It has not the right ring, because the impulse of a converted soul is to love, and not to be getting up and complaining of everyone else and finding fault.'

2. The Book further reminds us of the *fidelity love expects*: 'Love is strong as death' (8:6). There must be loyalty in love. True love is utterly dependable. That is why the marriage bond must always be regarded as so serious and so sacred. For a truly committed Christian, marriage must not be entered upon hurriedly or carelessly. It must be a matter of careful prayer. Only those who are deeply in love should consider it and there must be absolute trust on each side. Christians take the warning word of the apostle Paul about being unequally yoked (2 Cor. 6:14) very seriously indeed for they know that marriage with an unbeliever is likely to lead to tensions of various kinds and particularly in the problem of divided loyalties. A friend of mine and his wife had these words inscribed on the inside of their wedding rings: 'Each for the other and both for God.' That is exactly how it must be for those who are united in Christ.

3. *The Song of Solomon* makes several comments about the *responsibility love demands*. It emphasises the sacredness of love and insists that we 'stir not up nor awaken love until it please' (2:7; 3:5; 8:4). There have been in every generation those who think that love-making is a lighthearted game. They hold that it is something to be trifled with quite freely and casually and simply enjoyed as a physical experience without any sense of responsibility and dignity. But human emotions are quickly stirred and those who refuse to heed the warning-word of this book (2:7) will bring heart-ache and grief to others. That is not what God intended. Love was meant to bring immense delight and abiding joy to

all God's children and this is only possible in the context
of loyalty, trust and deep respect. In a time of declining
moral principles, Christians have the great privilege of
maintaining high standards about the sanctity of human
relationships. They know that His commandment is
that we should love as He loved (John 15:12). His love
was always enriching. It never brought any kind of unhappiness to anyone. This lofty standard and high ideal
must be ours also.

A Greater Miracle than the Exodus

AT this point in the Bible we come to three large prophetical books. The first of these prophets, Isaiah, has
been well described as 'the evangelical prophet'. He is
used by God to proclaim a message of serious warning
about man's sin and its awful effects in human life, but
this is followed by a superb account of God's merciful
act of deliverance and salvation.

The prophet Isaiah was called to his responsible task
in the same year as the death of King Uzziah. He
preached in the southern kingdom (Judah) at a time
when both northern and southern kingdoms were under
constant threat of invasion. The northern kingdom
(Israel) tried to strengthen itself by an alliance with
Syria and, when Judah refused to join this coalition, the
two nations came to Jerusalem to conquer it. Isaiah was
obviously well accepted at Court for he gave strong advice to the king in times of trouble.

Against this historical background of uncertainty,
tension and fear, Isaiah served as a prophet. The account
of how God spoke to him (6:1–8) is one of the most
helpful Old Testament passages about service and the
purity of life God expects of those who want to work for
Him.

The book of *Isaiah* can be divided into three main
sections:

1. REBELLION (Chapters 1–39)

In the first main section of the book Isaiah has a number of serious things to say about the *sin of man*. Chapter 1 outlines some of these and sin is described as *rebellion* (1 : 2), *ignorance* (1 : 3), *a heavy burden* (1 : 4), *sickness* (1 : 5–6). In their folly the people imagine that, even though their lives are so offensive to God, they may win His favour by the offering of their sacrifices (1 : 11–15). He longs to cleanse and forgive them (1 : 16–20) but they go on in their selfish sinning against other people (1 : 21–23) as well as against God (2 : 17–20). God's purpose for His people was that they might be a fruitful vine (5 : 1–7) but they were not bringing forth good fruit and so would have to be cut down or, to change the imagery, chastised and corrected. Isaiah knew that God was sovereign. The destiny of his nation was not in the hands of neighbouring monarchs and their armies but in the powerful hands of Almighty God. He told his king not to fear the threats of Israel and Syria (7 : 1–8 : 15) for he knew that the Assyrian nation, which they all dreaded, was also under the sovereign control of God. He was using that heathen country as the rod of His anger (10 : 5). In point of fact the northern kingdom fell (721 BC) to the Assyrian armies. Isaiah's predictions came true (8 : 3–8) and Judah itself became a tribute-state of Assyria.

All these distressing tensions of great national and political importance provided the framework of thought in which Isaiah discovered God's purpose to raise up a leader and deliverer for His people. But the leader was not destined to be the highly successful military captain or political overlord the people wanted. He was to be known as the Messiah, the chosen or anointed One, and

all these predictions do not find their fulfilment in a victorious war-lord but in the Lord Jesus Christ (9:2–7;
11:1–9). The people of Judah are told that, if their trust
is in God, they need not fear (12:1–2). He is with them
(12:6). Isaiah emphasises God's sovereignty not merely
over Judah but over all the nations (13:1–23:18). He
controls the forces of nature (24:1–27:13) let alone the
military movements of pagan kings. The present and the
future are all in His hands. 'Trust in God and enjoy the
peace He gives' is Isaiah's appeal to the troubled people
(26:3–4; 8:11–14; 12:2; 25:9; 33:2–6) but they often
refused to hear him and, in their panic, suggested forming political alliances in order to give themselves some
kind of security and confidence (30:1–7; 31:1–3). Isaiah
told them that this would be such a stupid thing to do.
God had spoken clearly to them through the prophet
that 'in quietness and in trust shall be your strength',
but they would not listen (30:15–16). Isaiah predicts
that a time will come when men will yield their total
allegiance to a King who will be a shelter to His people
(32:1–2), and when the righteous will be protected from
the onslaught of their enemies (33:15–22). He will prepare for them 'a way of holiness' (35:1–10) and the lives
of the blind, deaf, lame and dumb people will be
gloriously transformed. It is magnificent portraiture of
the Christian life and its many promises are to be
claimed by those who have acknowledged the kingship
(32:1) of the Lord Jesus Christ in their lives.

The closing chapters of the first section of the book
(36–39) turn from prophecy to history. They relate a
series of events in the reign of King Hezekiah, a good
king but fearful. The Assyrian armies beseiged Jerusalem
but God delivered His people. In His sovereign mercy
He also delivered Hezekiah from sickness. As we have

already seen (in a Book like *Esther*, for example) the Lord God is as concerned about the well-being of individuals as about the destiny of nations. But the closing words of this first main section (39 : 5–7) predict the subjugation of the nation by another nation, Babylon. This was to be God's way of chastising and purifying His wayward and rebellious people.

2. REDEMPTION (Chapters 40–55)

The second main section is addressed to an entirely different historical situation from that of Chapters 1–39. In order to understand the superb message of these later chapters we must interpret them in the light of a later period of Hebrew history. The Babylonian armies conquered the Assyrians and took their place as masters of the near-eastern world. True to Isaiah's prophecy (39 : 5–7) Judah was overrun and hundreds of its people were taken into captivity in Babylon. Chapters 40–55 portray a time when that exile was almost over. The rebellious people had been corrected (40 : 1–2). God had raised up another heathen conqueror who would in turn vanquish the Babylonians. His name was Cyrus, a previously insignificant tribal leader but a man whom God was to use to liberate His people from their captivity (41 : 2–4, 25; 44 : 28; 45 : 1–5). Here once again the prophet emphasises the sovereignty of God. He can use this pagan military genius even though he does not know God (45 : 4). Cyrus marched into Babylon only a few hours after its panic-stricken citizens had fled from the city carrying their idols on their pack-animals (46 : 1). With dramatic irony the prophet points out the difference between the faith of the Hebrew people and that of their oppressors: 'We do not have to make our God as the idol-manufacturers spend time and effort on

theirs' (40 : 18–20; 41 : 6–7; 44 : 9–20). Our God made us.
He is the eternal Creator (40 : 28–31; 51 : 13; 54 : 5). We
do not have to carry our God to safety. He carries us
(40 : 11; 46 : 3). The prophet views this act of mighty
saving deliverance as another 'exodus' like the miraculous release of the Jewish people from their slavery in
Egypt (43 : 15–21). Once again God is their Redeemer
(43 : 1–14). By His mighty invincible power He will
effect their redemption. They will be 'bought back' and
He will establish them again in their own land (51 : 3).

This section also looks away into the future in that
the prophet is inspired to portray the life and mission of
a 'servant' who will be called upon to suffer in the course
of his redemptive work. These special passages are
called 'The Servant Songs' (42 : 1–4; 49 : 1–6; 50 : 4–9
and 52 : 13–53 : 12). Several centuries after these magnificent words were written a traveller was reading these
very passages from the scroll of Isaiah. (We are told the
story in Acts 8). By that time, the Servant, the Lord
Jesus, had come into the world and had died to be the
Saviour of all who believe. The Ethiopian traveller was
joined by a Christian. As you read the story, you will
see that the early Christian people obviously believed
that these prophecies had been fulfilled in detail by the
Lord Jesus Christ, God's Son. He was the One who 'was
wounded for our transgressions' (53 : 4–6) and it is by
His saving death and victorious resurrection that we
obtain our redemption from sin. All we must do is turn
to Him in simple faith and turn *from* our sins. He will
pardon us (55 : 6–7) and transform us (55 : 12–13). Whatever He promises to do He has the power to effect. He
gives us His Word and that cannot fail us (55 : 8–11).

3. RESTORATION (Chapters 56–66)

The possible background to these closing chapters is the returned community, now settled back in Babylon. They are urged to keep the Sabbath as a sign of their obedience to God's Word and a token of their own personal holiness (56:1–5). Possibly by this time some of the people had replaced righteousness by materialism and God reminds them of the importance of obeying His Word about caring for the poor and hungry (58:1–12). There were those among the returned exiles who were grieving God (59:1–15) but the prophet anticipates better days for God's people when His glory will be manifest in the earth and His people will serve Him (60:1–66:24).

The prophecy of Isaiah covers an extended period of Jewish history but its message is for people of all times. Like the Jewish people (portrayed in Chapters 1–39) we have rebelled against God and refused to trust Him. While we were in the tyranny and bondage of our sin and shame He sent His Servant and Son to be our Redeemer (Chapters 40–55). Once we have received Him into our lives as our Saviour we must bring to Him our constant obedience (Chapters 56–66). He has great things in store for those who commit their lives fully to Him.

I

The Call of a Sensitive Youth

THE next book takes its name from a young country-lad, who was brought up at a place called Anathoth about three miles north of Jerusalem. He was probably born during the cruel reign of Manasseh but was called to be a prophet during King Josiah's reign. He then preached faithfully, although severely attacked, ridiculed and persecuted, until the fall of Jerusalem and the beginning of the Babylonian exile. It is not always an easy book to understand perhaps because its prophetic messages are not arranged in any chronological order. Some of Jeremiah's teaching cannot be precisely dated but his message was much the same throughout his ministry. When God called him (1 : 1–19), he did not want to obey. He probably guessed how difficult it was going to be and, quite naturally, he shrank from the task. Possibly the best way for us to outline the message of *Jeremiah*, in order to help in a first complete reading of the book, is to draw attention to his portraiture of *God*. Under the following three simple headings we ought to be able to summarise the leading aspects of Jeremiah's teaching.

1. THE FORSAKEN LOVER

It is quite probable that Jeremiah's first address in public was on this theme. The young prophet points out that after the Israelites left Egypt, the people relied utterly and completely upon God. During their wilderness wanderings they loved Him and depended on Him (2 : 1–7). But once they arrived in the Promised Land and settled down they forgot about God and started to live in a way which pleased them rather than in the way that honoured God. You may remember reading that very warning when we were studying the *Book of Deuteronomy* (e.g. Deut. 4 : 9; 8 : 11). Jeremiah was particularly grieved because even the priests, prophets and wise-men had forsaken God. They should have loved God most and been a rich example to the nation, but they were only out for their own selfish gain (2 : 8; 5 : 11–13; 6 : 13–14; 8 : 8–11; 14 : 13–16; 18 : 18; 23 : 9–40). They encouraged the people to believe that as long as they offered their sacrifices that was all that mattered. Jeremiah, as other prophets before him (e.g. Amos, Hosea, Micah, Isaiah) was used by God to say that their sacrifices were not acceptable unless they were the outward expression of utter devotion and sincere love (6 : 20; 7 : 21; 14 : 12). Although they went through this meaningless and mechanical ritual they were not pleasing God but grieving Him. In reality they had forsaken Him (2 : 13; 16 : 10–12; 17 : 13) and given their love to other gods (10 : 1–5, 14, 15; 11 : 9–10). The prophet constantly appeals to the people to return to the loving God they had left (3 : 12, 14, 22; 4 : 1, 14).

2. THE RIGHTEOUS JUDGE

Because He longed for His people to be His chosen instrument of blessing in the world, God knew that He had to chastise them and refine them. The only way He could accomplish this was to take many of them out of the land and away from the people whose idolatrous practices they had slowly assimilated into their own religious life (2 : 23–28; 7 : 16–20, 30–31; 8 : 19). The period they were in exile was to be used to purify them as a people and produce a refined remnant who were truly in love with God and who longed to walk in His way. God knew that there was no other way of making them into the people He wanted them to be (1:13–16; 5:14–19; 6:17–19, 22–30; 11:9–13). The prophet not only *said* the things that God had told him to proclaim (1:9) but he *did* certain things to demonstrate *in actions* what God's purpose was for the nation. We call this 'prophetic symbolism' and there are several vivid examples of this in *Jeremiah*. He made special use of this particular method of preaching in communicating to the people the truth that sin had spoilt them (13:1–11) and that only by an act of judgment (19:1–15) could they be re-made to God's original design (18:1–10).

3. THE UNIVERSAL KING

On the day when Jeremiah was called to his difficult task he was told that he was to be 'a prophet to the nations' (1:5–10). It was an early indication to the shy young countryman of God's sovereignty, and the closing section of the book is given over to a series of prophetic statements about the surrounding nations (Chapters 46:1–51:64). Jeremiah was deeply assured that God was not merely interested in Judah but in all nations. He was to use Nebuchadnezzar as his servant (25:9; 43:10) to work out His own predetermined purposes. The Babylonian king might well plan his detailed military manoeuvres but the destiny of God's people was not in his hands but in the hands of God. Jeremiah affirms that God's throne is 'set on high from the beginning' (17:12) and that is 'the place of our sanctuary'. He knew God to be the 'King of the Nations' (10:6–7).

Because God is the eternal King the welfare of His

chastised people would not be left to the mercy of the Babylonian kings. As a matter of fact, like all other empires, even that one would fall, magnificent though it was. As we have already seen in our study of *Isaiah*, Cyrus of Persia was to conquer the Babylonians and their capital city was to surrender without a fight. Although Jeremiah had this serious message of inevitable judgment and impending doom, his severe words were interspersed with others of radiant hope. Chapters 30–33 should be carefully studied in this respect. God not only threatened to hurl them out of the land (16:13), He also promised to bring them back (16:14–15; 24:4–7).

Jeremiah suffered for his faithfulness to God. He was hurt and grieved by his people's persistent sinfulness (8:18–9:2). He was persecuted by his own friends (11:18–23) and often felt terribly lonely (15:16–16:9). He was put into the stocks and left there all night (20:1–6). Because of the fierce opposition to this message he was occasionally tempted to keep quiet (20:7–9) but God's Word had so taken hold of him that he knew he had to speak. At times the hostility was so bad that he became extremely low in spirits and wished he had never been born (20:14–18). At different times he was brought before the authorities for trial (26:1–24), he was imprisoned (32:1–5; 33:1), he was beaten and subjected to a host of indignities (37:15; 38:4–13), and finally he was compelled against his will to go with a party of exiles to the country of Egypt (43:1–44:30). He was a courageous man who in dark days proved the truth of God's promise to fortify His servants (1:8, 17–19; 15:20) and constantly refresh them (17:7–8). If we begin some work for God we too are likely to encounter opposition, but the God who supported Jeremiah will strengthen us also.

A Sad Song with a Great Message

Lamentations is the name given to the next book in the Bible. Its setting and subject is the sad city of Jerusalem, helpless and bereft of any friends and helpers after its destruction by the armies of King Nebuchadnezzar of Babylon. This extended song, or group of songs, is a pathetic lament on the fall and desecration of the city in 586 BC. The city is movingly described as a lonely widow overwhelmed by her bitter grief (1 : 1–2) though there is a clear recognition throughout the book that the desolation is due to the sins of the people (1 : 8–10). The collapse of the temple, the ruined palaces and the broken walls are vividly described in a poem of great beauty (2 : 5–9). Even in a dirge like this God's sovereignty is mentioned. It has all happened because this was His purpose (2 : 17). This was a fire to purify them. He wants His people to recognise this, acknowledge their sins and seek Him in penitence (3 : 37–41). Rich and poor alike are under the judging hand of God (4 : 1–11; 5 : 11–14) and Jerusalem is no longer the place of exultant singing (5 : 15–18). It is recognised however that because God is merciful as well as sovereign, sinful man can return to Him (5 : 19–22). Those who seek Him will not be disappointed (3 : 21–26) for His steadfast love is renewed every single day of our lives. The main subject of *Lamentations* is obviously a sad one but its message is one of immense hope to all who feel remorseful, guilty and unclean. God wants to forgive.

Preacher to the Prisoners

IT would be quite wrong to create the impression that the Hebrew people who were taken into captivity were prisoners in our generally accepted sense of the term. They had a generous degree of freedom in Babylon and were encouraged to settle down in the land. Jeremiah sent a letter to the exiles and urged them to build houses, plant vineyards, bring up their families and seek not only their own well-being but also the welfare of the Babylonian cities where they were confined (Jer. 29:4-7). But although they were not convicts, they were captives. They were not free to return to their own land and in that sense they were 'imprisoned' within the vast country of Babylon. Many of them were intensely grieved (Psa. 137:1-6) and longed only to return to Jerusalem and their own country. Whatever the difficulties or hardships of His people, God never leaves them without a messenger and the man raised up by God to give a clear word of both correction and consolation to the exiles was Ezekiel.

This book is not easy for the beginner. We must remember that the beginning of exile was in two parts. First, in the year 597 a number of captives were taken away along with King Jehoiachin and later a further party were sent to Babylon in 586 after a further useless attempt to free themselves from the Babylonian oppression. Ezekiel went away with the first party (597). Some appear to have cherished the hope that this time of exile would be very brief. (Jer. 28 : 1-4). When he was called to the prophetic ministry, Ezekiel was given a vision of God in all His omnipotent glory. Many of the exiles may well have feared that Judah was God's land and now they were away from the land, how could they be sure that He was still with them? This opening vision (1 : 1-28) was of the chariot-throne of God surrounded by a rainbow, a sign to God's people of the reliability of His promises (Gen. 9 : 13). Through this magnificent first vision God was assuring the people as well as the prophet that He was with them in their sense of isolation and despair, and was in full control of world-events.

Ezekiel is composed of a series of visions and messages and in this book we have even more examples of 'prophetic symbolism' and the fascinating way the prophets communicated the truth by means of these 'action parables'. The book does not yield itself to any simple analysis and possibly the best way to understand the main aspects of the message is to study Ezekiel's teaching about God in much the same way as we did with *Jeremiah*. To this exilic prophet He is revealed in His omnipotence, holiness and compassion.

1. GOD IS OMNIPOTENT

As we have just seen, God rules and reigns over the whole world. He is not confined to the territories of Judah. The chariot-throne of God is manifested to His servant even in Babylon, the place of heathen darkness and spiritual despondency. Some of the exiles were naturally resentful that they had been taken from their homes but the prophet insists that the judgment of God still awaits those who remain in Jerusalem (12 : 1-28). Nothing can prevent it because all the unfolding events are in the hands of an omnipotent, all-powerful God.

God intended His people to be a fruitful vine (Isa. 5 : 1–7; Jer. 2 : 21; Psa. 80 : 8–16; Hos. 10 : 1) but they are fruitless and therefore useless. Ezekiel points out that even the wood of the vine cannot be used for pegs (15 : 1–8). It is only good for fuel and the omnipotent God has to correct them in the furnace of the exile-experience. Changing the imagery, Jerusalem is the unfaithful wife (16 : 1–63) and as such 'she' must be punished. Ezekiel vividly portrayed the siege of the city (24 : 1–14). The chastising hand of God cannot be averted. He alone knows that this refining process is essential if they are to be used in coming days. We have seen that both Isaiah and Jeremiah did not only speak to Judah but also to their heathen neighbours. Similarly Ezekiel as a prophet of the all-powerful sovereign God had things to say about pagan nations (25 : 1–32 : 32).

2. GOD IS HOLY

The holiness of God is a dominant theme in both *Isaiah* and *Ezekiel*. When God reveals Himself to the prophet he recognises that God is holy and falls on his face in reverent worship and humble submission (1 : 28). Ezekiel is grieved by the persistent idolatry of God's people. They refuse to recognise the holiness of God and they defile their own spiritual lives by setting up idols in their hearts. In one of his many visions the prophet is given insight into the sin of open idolatrous practice and secret idolatrous attitudes in the lives of many contemporary religious leaders (5 : 11; 6 : 1–7; 7 : 3–4; 8 : 1–18; 14 : 1–11; 20 : 1–39). The exile itself was to be used to rid God's people of these evil religious deeds or 'abominations' as Ezekiel frequently called them. There is a clear message here for us. It is easy for us to enthrone idols in our hearts (14 : 3). Anything is an idol if it comes between us and God. In his sovereignty God anticipates a time when all His people will serve Him with devoted holiness in a purified and prosperous land (chapters 40–48).

3. GOD IS LOVE

It is most important for us to see that whenever the prophets emphasise the inescapable nature of judgment their intention is to stress God's sovereign and determined purpose to bring His people back to Himself. He judged them because He loved them and wanted to use them (Amos 3:2; Prov. 3:11–12; Heb. 12:7–11). God's mercy is beautifully expounded in Ezekiel. He is the One who longs to pardon His sinful people (18:21–23, 30–32; 33:10–11). He is the Shepherd who searches for them because He loves them (34:11–16) and longs to bring them back. He is willing to cleanse them and give them a completely new heart (36:24–36). Dead as they are in their guilt and remorse, He is ready to fill them with new life and power (37:1–14).

The *Book of Ezekiel* is not all that easy to understand in places, but it yields rich treasures to those who will spend time over it.

Heroism in Dark Days

THE *Book of Daniel* belongs to a type of biblical literature which we call 'apocalyptic'. The word means 'un-
veiling' and the term describes books which reveal or
unveil the secrets of the future. *The Book of the Revelation* is the obvious New Testament example of this kind
of literature. *Daniel*'s message can be divided into two
quite distinct parts.

1. FIRM LOYALTY IN THE PAST (Chapters 1–6)

The first section describes the bravery and loyalty of
a group of Hebrew young men during the Babylonian
captivity. Daniel and his colleagues are given an important place at the heathen court and are expected to
eat certain foods which, in all probability, had first been
offered to pagan gods. In the thinking of the time those
who ate the food partook of the life of the deity, or com-
muned with the god. Daniel and his companions knew
that this would grieve God and, refusing to eat these
palace foods, lived on a simple vegetable diet. Yet God
prospered them and they were better in physical health
and intellectual wisdom than their fellow courtiers
(1:1–21). The story is told to lay stress at the very beginning of the book on the divine principle that God
clearly promises to honour those who honour and obey
Him (1 Sam. 2:30; Matt. 6:33).

Daniel and his loyal friends became renowned for
their wisdom (1:17) and early in the reign of King

Nebuchadnezzar he was used to interpret the meaning of a bewildering dream (2:1–49). Like most of the monarchs of the time, Nebuchadnezzar had extremely exalted notions of his own importance and maintained that everyone in his kingdom must do exactly what he ordered whether or not it was in conflict with their principles. He set up an image in the plain of Dura and demanded that everyone worship it; the penalty for refusing to do this was to be cast into a furnace and burnt to death. Daniel's friends, knowing that God's Word forbids idol worship (Exod. 20:4) refused to adore this image and they were accordingly cast into the fire. But, once again, God's promise to protect those who obey Him was wonderfully fulfilled and as they stood in the flames they were joined by one 'like the Son of God' (3:25, AV) and miraculously delivered (3:1–30). Daniel later had opportunity to help the bewildered king yet again with a further interpretation of a dream and Nebuchadnezzar was told that he was to be judged by God for his arrogant pride (4:1–37).

An outstanding incident in the life of a subsequent ruler, Belshazzar, is next recorded in the book (5:1–31) with its clear message about God's sovereignty and judgment and this story is followed by the famous one from the reign of Darius: Daniel in the lions' den. By this time, Daniel had become well-known at the Babylonian palace and several courtiers, jealous of his popularity, determined to lay a trap for him. A decree was made that no prayers were to be offered to any deity for a month—requests were only to be made to the king. Quite naturally, Daniel continued to pray to the Lord God three times every day and he was thrown into the lions' den as punishment (6:1–17). Once more the story records a miraculous deliverance (6:18–28). Daniel's

unshaken loyalty and spiritual courage was richly rewarded. It is possible that these great stories were of
immense spiritual encouragement during the later Mac-
cabean revolt, when many faithful Jews were severely
persecuted and tested for their faith. In later centuries,
they have also inspired thousands of dedicated Christian
people and given them fresh strength and fortitude
especially in difficult times.

2. FRESH LIGHT ON THE FUTURE (Chapters 7–12)
In our study of the *Book of Esther* we noted God's
fatherly concern for the individual as well as His
sovereign control over nations. In a similar way the
Book of Daniel expounds these two themes. God's
providential love in the lives of individual believers is
clearly illustrated in Chapters 1–6. The second half of
the book moves the scene from personal problems to
world affairs. In contrast to the first six chapters which
are mainly concerned with stories, the closing section
(Chapters 7–12) is given over almost entirely to visions.
These passages describe a series of dreams which Daniel
had, and they depict the unfolding scenes of world
history. Obviously, with this kind of literature there is
a difference of opinion about the interpretation of these
visions but the overall impression is not in the least
controversial : God reigns, He is in control of the destiny
of empires as well as individuals. In these chapters,
Daniel is clearly revealed not only as a man who is
enabled to see into the future but as a man of earnest
prayer (9:3–19). The closing chapter of the book portrays not the clash and conflict of world powers on this
earth, but man's destiny (12:2) and it reminds us of the
importance of searching our own hearts to ensure that
we are numbered among those who, because of simple

faith in Christ as Saviour of their lives, are 'written in the Book' (12 : 1), that is among those who are known to God as His children. These are described as those who 'purify themselves and make themselves white' (12 : 10) and in many places the Bible describes how such a miracle is possible (Psa. 51 : 1–2, 7; Isa. 1 : 16; Ezek. 36 : 25–27; 1 John 1 : 9).

A Marriage Breakdown and its Message

WITH the prophecy of *Hosea*, we come to the first of the twelve books known as 'The Minor Prophets'. They are described as 'minor' not because they are of secondary importance but because of their brevity when compared with much longer books such as *Isaiah*, *Jeremiah* and *Ezekiel*.

One of the difficulties about the prophetical books is that they do not claim to have been placed in the Bible in chronological order, so we shall need to remind ourselves in each case of the historical background. Sometimes the precise date of a prophet's ministry is given in an opening verse, but in some cases we are not given this extremely useful information and in that event we have to try to discern this detail from the prophet's message.

Hosea was one of the most attractive prophets of Old Testament times. He was a northerner and preached to his own people in the northern kingdom (Israel) prior to its downfall and collapse. He is one of a group we sometimes call 'the eighth-century prophets' which also includes Amos, Micah and Isaiah. You will remember from our readings in the Historical Books that the northern territories were overrun by the Assyrian armies and its capital city of Samaria fell in 721 BC after one of the longest and most dreadful sieges in history.

Before these momentous events, Hosea was given the task of re-calling Israel to God and he did so in a most eloquent manner and with a deeply sensitive and passionate appeal. He was extremely gifted as an artist *in words* and painted some vivid pictures of a loving God and His mercy towards His stubborn, rebellious children.

The book touches on a number of highly important prophetic themes and constantly returns to these, frequently reiterating a message by presenting it in a fresh way and with the aid of different word-pictures. For this reason it is not possible to analyse the book chapter by chapter into a group of clear divisions and it is probably more helpful to draw attention to some of its leading themes. Perhaps we might take as our starting point one of Hosea's most graphic sayings: 'gray hairs are sprinkled upon him, and he knows it not' (7:9). With the aid of this vivid imagery Hosea is saying that the spiritual and moral life of the nation has seriously declined, that they are rather like the person who is utterly unaware of his first grey hairs! What were the signs of decline which Hosea had so perceptively observed in the life of his people?

1. BROKEN VOWS

The key term in *Hosea* is variously rendered in our English versions as mercy, kindness, steadfast love, loving kindness. It translates a Hebrew word (hesed) meaning 'covenant love'. God loved His people deeply and they were bound to Him in a covenant relationship, like a marriage. But they had gone after other lovers and broken their vows of covenant love and loyalty. Hosea did not merely preach about these issues as cold doctrinal facts. He knew something of how God must have felt, for his own wife had done much the same as the nation of Israel. She had left him and his children and gone after other lovers (1 : 1–2 : 13). George Adam Smith said of Hosea : 'His grief became his gospel.' But, just as Hosea went after his wife in the hope of winning her back, so God was pleading with His people to return to Him (2 : 14–23). The prophet's wife had fallen into awful degradation and he had to buy her back as a slave from her life of harlotry and adultery, but he did this eagerly and willingly because he loved her so deeply (3 : 1–5). This tragedy in his own marriage became a parable of God's grief over his loveless children. They too had become harlots by going after other gods (4 : 11–5 : 4).

2. Useless Leaders

One of the grave difficulties which the eighth-century prophets had to face was the serious moral failure of many contemporary prophets and priests. Men who ought to have been a rich spiritual example to their fellow-countrymen were spiritually decadent and corrupt (4 : 1–10). Moreover, Hosea insisted that the kings of the northern kingdom could never be helpful leaders from a spiritual point of view. He knew that it was never God's purpose for the land to be divided between north and south, Israel and Judah. His intention was that all his people should live together in a united kingdom under devout kings who were of the line of David. They could not hope for spiritual prosperity when they were serving the wrong kind of rulers (3 : 4–5; 7 : 3–7; 8 : 4; 10 : 7; 13 : 10–11).

3. Wrong Friends

In their weakness the leaders of the northern kingdom turned for help from their heathen neighbours. Though they were in many respects materially and economically

K

prosperous, God had brought them low. Afraid of invasion by a mighty enemy they tried to fortify themselves and strengthen their position by forming alliances with other countries. All the prophets regarded this kind of procedure as a clear indication of lack of trust in God and it was viewed as the most serious outward expression of disobedience and apostasy (5 : 13–14; 7 : 8–16; 8 : 8–10; 12 : 1; 14 : 3).

4. CORRUPT WORSHIP

What grieved the prophets of this period most was the fact that while all this apostasy was going on there was no shortage of sacrifices and offerings on the altars of both kingdoms, but it was not offered to the Lord God as an expression of deep gratitude and overflowing love. The spiritual life of the nation had become contaminated by religious practices which they had taken over from the Canaanites who lived in the land before they arrived. These included all manner of degrading rituals and ceremonies including 'sacred prostitution'. Worship was being offered to Baal, the god of the land, who was worshipped by the Canaanite people. If there was a particularly good harvest the Israelites attributed this generous favour to Baal rather than to the Lord God who had brought them into the Promised Land (2 : 8–13; 7 : 14–16; 8 : 11–13; 10 : 1–10; 11 : 1–2).

Yet, despite all their stubborn rebellion and depravity, God loved them. He had shown His love long ago by bringing them out of Egyptian slavery (11 : 1, 3). Even though they grieved Him, He could not possibly give them up (11 : 8–9). He longed for them to return to Him. Just as the prophet himself had done all within his power to recover his wife from her sin and degradation, so God was begging Israel to return to Himself (14 : 1–2). He desired *steadfast or covenant love* (hesed) and not sacrifice (6:6). If they would come back to Him in deep sincerity then they would be forgiven (14:2) and healed (14:4), and God would establish them and prosper them in all their ways (14:4–7).

Hosea's message to Israel is most relevant in our own lives. Sometimes Christian people lose their 'first love' as the Christians did in the church at Ephesus (Rev. 2:4). We break our promises of love. This sometimes happens because, like the Israelites of Hosea's time, we become involved with the wrong friends. When we lose our love for God, our attendance at Sunday worship and even our daily Bible reading and prayer can quickly degenerate into mechanical ritual. God's love is so great that He longs that we might return to Him. He often hedges up our paths so that like the people of the northern kingdom we are driven into His presence (2:6–15) to find pardon, restoration and renewed joy.

A Chance to Begin Again

IT is hardly possible to give a precise date to the *Book of Joel*. It comes next in the minor prophets but they obviously do not appear in the Old Testament in exact chronological order. The prophecy itself does not give us any detail which helps to fix it in an accurate historical setting, so some scholars have given it a very early date while others have suggested that it belongs to a period well after the Exile. It is probably best to regard Joel as one of the earliest of the minor prophets. He may well have preached in the southern kingdom during the reign of King Joash, but we cannot be certain. In this case the exact date of the prophet's ministry does not matter very much and our ignorance about his times certainly does not create any difficulties about interpreting his message.

Joel's teaching is focused on two favourite prophetic themes:

1. CORRECTIVE PUNISHMENT

The prophetic word is occasioned by a severe plague of locusts which created havoc in the Judean farmlands. It appears to have been one of the worst plagues of its kind and these ruthless little creatures had pretty well devoured everything in the land (1 : 1–12). Joel saw this not as a mere freak of circumstance or a natural misfortune; he regarded it as the judgment of God. The prophet called on the people to set time aside for fasting in order to give time for prayer and repentance (1 : 14–20). Serious as this national calamity was, Joel viewed it almost as a type of an even more terrible judgment that awaited those who are finally impenitent (2 : 1–11). Like the other prophets he believed that God must ultimately intervene in world affairs and this dramatic sovereign intervention was known by them as 'the Day of the Lord'.

2. CONDITIONAL PROMISE

God is merciful as well as just. He pleads with His people to return to Him (2 : 12–29), but their penitence must be genuine and sincere. 'Rend your hearts and not your garments' (2 : 13). God makes a promise that He will restore the years which the locusts have eaten (2 : 25). He will make good the devastation of former years. It is a wonderful promise, and truly penitent people over the intervening centuries have rejoiced in its merciful provision. Sometimes we feel overwhelmed by guilt and grief. We wish we had not sinned and brought heartache to others as well as bitter disappointment and despair upon ourselves. Yet God, in his grace, mercy and steadfast love (2 : 13) will not only forgive us but help to redeem the situation by bringing some good out of the devastation and sadness. We must note though that as well as being a merciful promise, it is a *conditional* one. If we want to experience His restoring mercy in our lives, we must bring our sincere repentance to Him.

In the closing section of the book, the prophet Joel shares his confidence in God's sovereignty. He not only controls the life and history of His own people, but shapes the destiny of all the nations. All of them are finally answerable to Him (2 : 30–3 : 21).

Joel's message to Judah was not only for that nation

in its despair but for all who feel that they have grieved God. It begs us to seek His pardon (2:12–13). If we do so in sincerity, we shall receive His provision (2:18–27) and experience His power (2:28–29). The New Testament apostles saw the fulfilment of this promise at Pentecost (Acts 2:17–21). The Spirit who came upon those truly penitent men powerfully equipped them for valiant service. He will do the same for us.

The Shepherd who had to Preach

THE Old Testament prophets were rarely popular with contemporary religious and national leaders. There were men like Isaiah who had easy admission to the royal palace but they were the exception rather than the rule. Amos and Jeremiah are far more typical. They were bitterly opposed by the religious leaders of their times (Amos 7 : 10–17; Jer. 20 : 1–2). In one such hostile encounter, Amos told the leading priest at the Bethel sanctuary that he was not a professional prophet who was making a living out of this kind of work (7 : 14). He explained to Amaziah that he was employed as a herdsman but the Lord had called him quite unmistakably to this prophetic ministry and He had sent him to preach to the rebellious people of the northern kingdom. Amaziah told him to go back home to Judah and do his preaching there (7 : 12) but Amos was only preaching at Bethel and in similar towns in Israel because God had thrust him forth and the herdsman knew that he could not possibly resist *that* order or disobey such a clear command (3 : 7–8).

The preaching of Amos was blunt, radical and entirely uncompromising and, as such, it was bound to be unpopular with the majority. The fact that he came from Tekoa in the southern kingdom would make it even more unacceptable. The Israelites could not even rely on local patriotism to temper the harsh sayings. From even a cursory reading of the book it becomes clear that

Amos must have been a fiery, uninhibited type of man, completely fearless and attractively courageous. He was commissioned to preach a stern and direct message at a time of economic prosperity in the northern kingdom. Possibly, as he looked after his flock, he quietly reflected on some of the great themes of the Law—God's holiness, justice and mercy. He may have met travellers on the great trade routes which bordered on his pasture-lands and from these he would hear of the tragic corruption in the moral and religious life of Judah and Israel and also of the inhumanity of other nations. It is quite likely that his own work would occasionally demand a visit to the market places of the northern kingdom and here he would see for himself how low the nation was spiritually.

Probably leaving his flock in the care of someone else and finding it hard to believe that God's call to take up work as a prophet was for the rest of his life, Amos set out for the busy centres of population in Israel. The prophets had to capture the attention of their audience and Amos had a brilliant way of collecting a crowd. He started to talk about the sins of other nations! The people soon gathered around him. It is always easier to criticise the sins of others than face up to our own and Amos knew that by preaching about their neighbour's cruelties he would soon have a congregation (1 : 1–2 : 5). They would heartily agree with the prophet's firm convictions that such sins would be punished by a just God, little realising that he was about to add them to the list of offenders (2 : 6–16). Amos made it clear that the fact they were God's chosen people did not exempt them from punishment. Far from it. Because He loved them He wanted to use them, and if they were to be used then they must be cleansed from sin. 'You only have I known of all the families of the earth; therefore I will punish you for all your iniquities' (3:2). That word 'known' is one of the most tender and intimate Old Testament terms. It describes the closest possible relationships. It does not refer to a merely intellectual knowledge. In Hebrew thought a man 'knew' his wife. Amos was saying that God was closer to them than to any other people in the world and punishment was a necessary prelude to purity. Amos knew that this kind of message would not go down well. God had spoken clearly to him (3:3–7) and when the Lord God had revealed His truth 'who can but prophesy?' (3:8).

Amos discerned at least three grievous sins in the life of the nation:

1. CRUELTY
'They sell the righteous for silver, and the needy for a pair of shoes—they . . . trample the head of the poor into the dust of the earth, and turn aside the way of the afflicted' (2:6–7). The prophet realised that although Israel was enjoying a period of comparative prosperity, the few who were rich had been made so at the expense of the poor. The wealthy citizens of the northern kingdom cared little for the welfare of those who were without money, adequate clothing and necessary food. The prophet had severe things to say to those who 'oppress the poor and crush the needy' (4:1). Some of the rich people had several houses (3:15; 5:11) while the poor lived in hovels. They gave lavish parties and entertained each other at extravagant banquets but did not care about those of their own nation who had to spend their days begging for bread (6:4–6).

2. UNREALITY

With biting sarcasm Amos referred to the multiplicity of their sacrifices and like other prophets told the people that unless their sacrifices were offered in loving adoration God did not want them (4:4–5). The prophet told them to seek God Himself rather than chase off to famous shrines where they could present their unacceptable offerings (5:4–5). God required a different kind of offering from His people in their present circumstances. He wanted them to present the 'sacrifice' of righteous living and just dealings with their fellows (5:21–27). Anyone with money could offer an animal sacrifice but that was of no use to God if their lives were corrupt.

3. DISHONESTY

The message of Amos was not only about the sins of the rich homes in Israel but of the dishonest practices in the markets of the northern kingdom. The traders used false weights in their scales and robbed many an innocent customer (8:4–6). Those responsible for the administration of justice were also corrupt. They accepted bribes and freely indulged in all kinds of fraudulent practice (5:10–15). Justice was perverted and, as the wealthy people of the land gained more and more influence and control, those who lacked money were ground more and more into the dust (2:7). It is a pathetic story of man's inhumanity to man. When God is not given His rightful place in men's hearts, all sense of the dignity of human life is lost.

It will be clearly seen from all this that Amos realised how widespread was the sin of Israel. It affected their social relationships, degraded their religious practices, perverted their economic transactions and corrupted their legal proceedings. Homes, sanctuaries, market-stalls and simple law-courts ('the gate' was the place where legal controversies were settled in near-eastern communities) had all become depraved and degraded. What was the answer to this immense problem? God revealed His purposes to the prophet in a series of *five visions* (Chapters 7–9) in which it was made plain that these sins must be punished in order that God's people might be completely purified. When Amos made direct statements like 'the sanctuaries of Israel shall be laid waste and I will rise against the house of Jeroboam with the sword' (7:9), we are hardly surprised that the leading priest at one of the king's sanctuaries told the prophet to go home! The prophet could not be so easily silenced. He had a great burden for God's people and although his message was stark and stern, it was not lacking in compassion and earnest appeal. He told them how God had tried time and again to bring His people back to Himself but the sad refrain is constantly repeated, 'Yet you did not return to me, says the Lord' (4:6, 8, 9, 10, 11).

The word of Amos about God's judgment was certainly fulfilled. The capital city of Samaria fell to the Assyrians (721 BC) and the whole countryside was ravaged by their cruel armies. As Isaiah made it plain later, God was using that pagan nation as the rod of His anger. (Isa. 10:5; Amos 5:1–4, 16–20; 6:14; 7:9, 11; 8:1–3). When Amos prophesied, his word was rejected (7:12–13) but he told of a time when, in their distress, God's people would long for the word of God (8:11–12). If God speaks to us about wrong things in our lives we would be foolish to resist His appeal or disobey His commands. He only corrects us in order to make us more useful (John 15:2).

A Straight Word about Justice

THROUGH the centuries God's people have been cruelly opposed. The Old Testament contains many stories of severe persecution and bitter distress. They suffered at the hands of their Egyptian overlords (Exod. 1:1–14) and once they got into the Promised Land they found themselves surrounded by opposing nations. Possibly the most hostile of their neighbours were the Edomites. They dealt with Judah in a most malicious way and the bad feeling between the two countries went back over many centuries. Although they were the descendants of Esau, and so bound to God's people by a tie of kinship, the Edomite people refused to let the Hebrew people go through their territory when they were on their journey to Canaan (Deut. 23:7–8; Num. 20:14–21). This obviously made for bad relations between the two peoples and once the Jews became established in the land under the leadership of their own king the hostility grew. Several stories are told in the historical books of the strife between both countries (2 Sam. 8:13–14; 1 Kings 11:14–25; 2 Kings 8:20–22; 14:7–10). Amos also knew of their cruelty and oppression (Amos 1:11–12).

The *Book of Obadiah* focuses on what was probably the severest blow the Edomites could inflict on the people of Judah. The terrible time came when Nebuchadnezzar's armies attacked and captured the city of Jerusalem. The Edomite tribesmen helped in the greedy plundering, mocked the plight of the captives as they made their sad journey to Babylon and then made frequent attacks on the poor and dispirited minority left behind in Judaea (Obad. 10–14; Psa. 137; Lam. 4:21–22; Ezek. 25:12–14).

The short prophetic message of Obadiah is proclaimed not in revenge but in the deep spiritual conviction that God has His hand upon His people even in times when they feel depressed and forsaken. He rules the world in justice. The Edomites are answerable to him for all their atrocities. The closing section of the book (verses 15–21) predicts the ultimate restoration of God's people, when 'the house of Jacob shall possess their own possessions' (17) completely untroubled by avaricious neighbours. It says something to us about leaving our distresses in God's sovereign hands. The true Christian does not take revenge on those who oppose him or act unjustly or unkindly towards him (Rom. 12:14–21). He leaves such matters to the God who is utterly just and loving.

The Prophet who Ran Away

THE story of Jonah belongs to a time when the powerful Assyrian Empire was beginning to show signs of decline. Jonah was called to a difficult task. He lived in the long reign of King Jeroboam II of Israel (2 Kings 14:25) and he knew only too well the cruelty of the Assyrians. They were well known throughout all the near eastern world for their horrible atrocities towards their opponents. Most Hebrews looked forward to a time when God would punish them for these cruelties, but Jonah heard a clear call from God to journey to the huge Assyrian city of Nineveh to urge that godless nation to repent. Like most of the Jews at that time, Jonah did not want them to repent; he wanted them to perish! God does not always call us to deliver the message *we* like.

Jonah rebelled and the story of God's gentle dealings with his stubborn servant form the substance of the next book of the minor prophets. It is sad that doubts about the historical details in the story have tended to obscure its message. Once Jonah's name is mentioned, the main topic for discussion is whether a man could possibly survive if swallowed by a whale. Actually the story in *Jonah* does not mention a whale. It says that God prepared 'a great fish' (1:17). Once we deny the possibility of the miraculous we surely depreciate the message and value of the Bible and, more seriously, question the power of God. If we try to explain away all the miracles of the Old Testament what shall we do when we come to the stupendous miracles of New Testament times such as the resurrection of Christ? How can a corpse come to life again but by a miraculous intervention on the part of Almighty God? To return to the Jonah narrative, there are, as a matter of fact, one or two stories of human beings who have survived after being swallowed by whales. In his book *The Cruise of the Cachalot* Frank Bullen tells us that when a sperm whale is about to die it throws up the entire contents of its stomach. Bullen actually saw this happen and said that the amount of solid matter which was ejected reached huge proportions. At the end of the last century a man called James Bartley who worked on the whale ship *Star of the East* was swallowed by a whale somewhere near the Falkland Islands. The fish was killed and after the crew spent many hours dissecting it, Bartley was recovered alive.

We have already observed, however, that this is not the main point of the Jonah story. It is a superb example of the missionary message of the Old Testament. God's compassion was so great that even the cruel Ninevites must have an opportunity to hear of His offer of pardon and mercy. Jonah did not want to give them this kind of hope so he boarded a ship which was going in the opposite direction (1:3). We are sometimes guilty of this same kind of disobedience. God has His own way of bringing us back into line with His will. The prayer of Jonah (2:1–9) is a magnificent psalm of dependence, confession and trust. In his grief, the disobedient prophet believed he had been cast out of the Lord's presence (2:4) but God delivered him so that he could proclaim salvation to the Assyrians (2:10–3:4). The Ninevite citizens listened attentively to the serious things the prophet had to say and they turned to God in deep penitence (3:5–10). Very few of the Old Testament prophets had the joy of seeing results from their preaching. Jeremiah and Ezekiel were both told that hardly any of the people who heard them would respond to their message (Jer. 7:27; Ezek. 3:7). Jonah was one of the few to get an immediate response when he preached but, instead of being thrilled, he was utterly despondent. He did not want the Ninevites to be forgiven. He had a narrow and severely restricted view of what God could do. He told God he wished he could die (4:2–5). The prophet said he would rather die himself than live to see the repentant Ninevites live! Yet just as God was merciful to the penitent Assyrians, so He was patient with his rebellious prophet. By means of a simple 'parable of nature' (4:6–11) He pleaded with Jonah to think graciously and generously even of those who had been his enemies. The Jonah story is a magnificent reminder of God's merciful provision for those who are truly repentant, and of the persistent correction He exercises towards those of His servants who do not obey His voice and proclaim His mercy.

Trouble on the Horizon

LIKE Isaiah, the prophet Micah was called to preach to the citizens of the southern kingdom (Judah) in the eighth century BC. These two men addressed an identical situation of religious and moral decay in the life of their nation, though it is fascinating to see how they looked at it from slightly different points of view. Isaiah appears to have been a leading citizen of Jerusalem. He was certainly well-known at the royal court and probably came from some high ranking Judaean family. He saw the evils of the nation from the standpoint of a city-dweller, whereas Micah was essentially a countryman. He belonged to Moresheth-gath, a small town north of Jerusalem, in the lowlands of Judaea and he looked at the plight of the nation from the viewpoint of one who was accustomed to rural life.

The message of the *Book of Micah* can be divided into two parts:

1. GOD'S COMPLAINT (Chapters 1–3)

The opening chapters of the book focus our attention on three important themes in Micah's preaching.

(i) *Idolatrous Worship*

'All her images shall be beaten to pieces' (1:7). Micah lived quite near to the Israelite border and he knew about the idolatry of those spiritually corrupt northern cities. Their religious sanctuaries were no longer given

L

over to the worship of the only true God. Deeply sincere worship had been replaced by all manner of corrupt practices, many of them morally degrading, but all done in the name of religion. In a graphic saying Micah portrays the Lord God marching in judgment into Judah's equally defiled territories (1:2–4). As he went from town to village Micah fearlessly proclaimed this message of impending doom, and yet passionately appealed to them for a genuine change of heart. He used very similar language to Isaiah when he described the sin of Judah as an incurable wound (1:9, cf. Isa. 1:5–6).

(ii) Inevitable Judgment

In the second part of the first chapter, Micah vividly portrays the invading armies sweeping over the Judaean hills and ravaging all the various townships and rural communities. We have already observed that the Old Testament prophets had to use all kinds of different devices to capture the attention of apathetic congregations and to fix their unpopular message in the minds of the people. Micah used a series of puns to drive home his urgent message to these indifferent groups of people in the towns and cities of Judaea. The force of these puns, or 'verbal fireworks' as one Old Testament scholar has called them, is brought out in Dr Moffatt's translation of Micah 1:10–11:

> Weep tears at Tear town (Bochim),
> Grovel in the dust at Dustown (Beth-ophrah)
> Fare forth stripped, O Fairtown (Saphir!)
> Stirtown (Zaanan) dare not stir.

This kind of word-play was used to communicate his message forcefully to the spiritually careless people he met as he travelled through all these towns and villages. Micah was out to get them to face these serious spiritual realities but instead they tried to evade the persistent and pleading voice of God.

(iii) *Iniquitous Rulers*

The landowners and merchants were utterly indifferent to the moral demands of God's law. 'They covet fields, and seize them; and houses, and take them away; they oppress a man and his house, a man and his inheritance' (2 : 2). In the thinking of the prophets there was no distinction between sacred and secular, nor between what was religious and what was moral. Both belonged together. Men must be righteous because God is righteous. They must be holy because He is holy. Similarly because God loved His people and provided for them, so they must care for the widow, the orphan, the alien and the poor. This was one of the important aspects of the Law of Moses (Exod. 22 : 21–24, Deut. 24 : 17–22). To disobey this commandment was to grieve the God who loved all His people equally. The ruling classes were singled out for special condemnation by the prophet. He knew that many of them had to administer the simple judicial system in the land but they were accepting bribes and justice was being perverted in all parts of the country (3 : 1–3, 9–12). Prophets and priests were equally self-seeking and avaricious (2 : 5–7, 11–12). They would give a good message to a man who paid them well but they did not seek a true word from God's mouth. Money was all that mattered to them.

2. God's Appeal (Chapters 4–7)

We must not run away with the impression that Micah's message was all about judgment. He told the people of a time when, far from giving themselves up to idol worship, God's people would offer acceptable and genuine worship at Jerusalem (4:1–2). In those days there would be no threat of invasion and warfare (4:3–5) and those who had been chastised and refined would return to the land (4:6–8). The prophet knew that the necessary period of correction in exile would come to an end and God would eventually restore His people to their own country (4:9–5:1). In contrast to his own times when the rulers were so godless and greedy, arrogant and assertive, Micah looked forward to a time when a perfect Ruler would be born in the humble setting of a small Judaean town, Bethlehem (5:2–4). This magnificent prophecy was fulfilled, of course, in the birth of the Lord Jesus Christ. Micah knew that a remnant of God's people would be faithful to Him and he reminded them of the glories of the perfect age which was to come for all God's faithful ones under the leadership of their Messiah (5:5–15).

Against this background of hope and encouragement the prophet pleaded with the people of the southern kingdom to return to the Lord. God had a controversy with them, a serious difference of opinion. Had He let them down in some way, failed them or neglected them, that they had gone to other gods (6:1–5)? God told them what kind of worship was acceptable to Him (6:6–8), but instead of pleasing Him by behaving justly towards their fellow men, many of the traders were dishonest and deceitful (6:9–7:6). Micah knew that the only way God could purify His people was by the chastisement and anguish that would come to them in the exile (7:7–14) but in it all He would be sovereign, using heathen nations for His own corrective purposes (7:15–17). His message is brought to a moving climax in one of the most compassionate appeals of the Old Testament. Their pardoning God would cast the sins of His repentant people into the depths of the sea. His promises would not fail. (7 : 18–20).

Micah's message is still relevant. We sometimes forget that God is just as concerned about what happens at our work as at our worship. Mondays are of equal importance as Sundays. If we grieve Him in one area in our lives we offend Him in all. Sometimes He has to take seemingly harsh measures to bring us to the place where we honestly face our sins and ask for His pardon.

The End of a Cruel Nation

THE teaching contained in the *Book of Nahum* concerns the fate of Nineveh. It was to this same Assyrian city that Jonah had been sent in the previous century with God's generous offer of merciful pardon. Had Jonah been commissioned to deliver the truths contained in *Nahum*, he would have gone without a murmur! Its message is one of inevitable judgment and inescapable doom for the heathen people. From the start of the eleventh century BC the Assyrians constantly sent their huge armies into the west intent on fierce military attack and merciless subjugation. During the whole time of their ascendency in the near-east the Assyrian armies behaved in a most cruel manner towards any nation which cared to protect itself from their onslaughts. Nahum makes vivid mention of those dreaded columns of powerful Assyrian chariots, and the obvious fear they brought to any small nation which could not possibly match such unrivalled military strength. (2:3–4, 3:2–3). The vicious way they dealt with their opponents is recorded in their own annals. For example, their King Ashur-nasir-pal invaded a certain city under the governorship of a man called Khulai and the Assyrian victor records his conquest in the following words:

'Six hundred warriors I put to the sword; three thousand captives I burned with fire; I left not a single one among them alive to serve as hostages. Khulai, their governor, I captured alive. Their corpses I piled in heaps; their young men and maidens I burned in the fire; Khulai, their governor, I flayed and his skin I spread upon the wall of the city of Damdamusa; the city I destroyed, I ravaged, I burned with fire.'

All this kind of cruelty must be borne in mind when we read the prophetic message of Nahum. The northern kingdom had fallen to the Assyrians and Judah itself lived in fear of this same invader. No wonder Nahum almost leaps with rapturous joy at the prospect of their downfall. Almost the entire book is given to this single theme, but as well as singing with exultant delight at the thought of Assyria's final collapse, the prophet has some inspiring insights into the nature of God. They are worthy of special note as we read the book:

1. THE JUSTICE OF GOD

'The Lord is slow to anger and of great might, and the Lord will by no means clear the guilty' (1:3). The Old Testament prophets believed that God had set man in a moral universe. Those who offend God by cruelty to their fellows must ultimately be punished for their godless inhumanity. Man cannot treat his fellow man just as he wishes and hope to get away with it. It is important in this connection to note that the prophets were not merely concerned about acts of cruelty and oppression towards Israel and Judah. Cruelty *anywhere* was distasteful to God. He loved all men and would not allow evil of any kind to go unnoticed and unpunished. Some of the sins of Israel's neighbours which Amos condemned were not necessarily against the northern kingdom but against other equally pagan nations (Amos 2:1 and possibly 1:6 and 1:9). God was not only interested in the welfare of the Jews.

2. THE POWER OF GOD

Nahum also offered rich encouragement to God's people. He knew how often they had to take refuge from the cruel Assyrian armies and against this military background they were reminded that 'The Lord is good, a stronghold in the day of trouble; He knows those who take refuge in Him' (1:7). Although His people might often be in serious difficulties, God would not abandon them to their enemies. He would fortify them and deliver them.

3. THE SOVEREIGNTY OF GOD

Like Isaiah (40:15–17, 22–23) Nahum believed that all the nations of the world were under God's omnipotent control. He could boldly address the Assyrians, therefore, in strong convinced terms such as these: 'The Lord has given commandment about you: "No more shall your name be perpetuated" ' (1:14). The prophet knew that Assyria's 'unceasing evil' (3:19) was about to be punished, for God was on the throne of world history. He had issued His commandment concerning their destiny. God was not a mere tribal deity, interested only in his own restricted territories. He was the Judge of *all* the earth (Gen. 18:25) for He was its Creator and also its King.

A View from the Tower

ONE of the most fascinating aspects of these prophetic books of the Old Testament is that we are not only confronted with what these great men *said* for God but we can also observe how the prophets themselves reacted to God's Word when first they received it. Isaiah's vision (Isa. 6:1 ff), Jeremiah's call and the many later conversations he had with God (Jer. 1:4–19; 8:18–9:2; 15:10–21), Ezekiel's initial reaction to God's revelation (Ezek. 1:28–3:27) are just a few examples of this feature of the prophetic writings. The *Book of Habakkuk* records a dialogue between the prophet and his God. It is not so much a summary of what Habakkuk preached about as a record of his conversation with the Eternal God. There is no date assigned to the book in its opening verse and we know nothing about the prophet apart from what is contained within these three chapters. In that the Chaldean victories are mentioned (1:6–10) the most likely date is after the collapse of the Assyrian empire. Nineveh fell to the Babylonians (612 BC) as Nahum had predicted. Habakkuk's statement about the Babylonian triumphs (1:6–10) suggests that the date of this prophecy is probably during a time of increasing military success for that nation, possibly between 626 and 605 BC.

Habakkuk's problem is that the people of Judah are living in arrogant sinfulness. The prophet has prayed that God would intervene in some way, for the nation stubbornly refuses to obey God's Word and the land is full of social disorder and appalling injustice. But, despite the prophet's plea, God does not seem to answer his prayers (1 : 1–4). Habakkuk is then told that God will be using the Babylonians to chastise God's people (1 : 5–11) but this baffles the prophet. How can God use an evil nation to execute His judgment on the people of God? Surely that is not right (1 : 12–17)! Bewildered and troubled about the message God has given him he waits upon God (2 : 1). Every Hebrew community had its watch-towers. They were placed at strategic positions on the city walls so that the appointed watchmen could look out for approaching danger (see Ezek. 3 : 17–21, 33 : 1–9), Habakkuk uses the expression figuratively. He too is going to the watch-tower to see what God's message is going to be to him and, therefore, what he is to communicate to the people. God tells him that the message he is commissioned to deliver must be made unmistakably clear to them so that 'he may run who reads it' (2 : 2) or 'one may read it at a glance' as Dr Moffatt translates it. In short the message is that although God is to use the Babylonians for His purposes, they will ultimately bring ruin upon themselves; in this way they too will be chastised by God. The Babylonian pride is contrasted with the faithfulness (2 : 3–5) of God's people. This 'faithfulness' has been described as man's response to God's faithfulness. It is the firm belief that God will be utterly true to His own nature and do what is absolutely right and just.

A series of 'woes' follow in the book (2 : 6–19), these being the taunts of others as they see the final collapse and utter ruin of the nation which has been such a severe oppressor. The prophet affirms his confidence in the absolute sovereignty of God and His unhindered sway over all the world (2 : 20).

The final chapter is a song of triumphant thanks-giving (3 : 1–19). It vividly portrays the victorious march of God through His own world as He comes to the aid of His own people (3 : 1–15). But all this is a psalm of faith for as yet the Babylonians have not been punished by the Lord God. They still have their corrective work to do in the life of God's people. Therefore the prophet has to 'quietly wait' upon the God who will not fail His own (3 : 16). The book closes with a superb illus-tration of how a man can pray if he relies upon the faithfulness of God (3.17–19). The prophet says that even if there is no harvest and the land is stricken with severe famine yet he will rejoice in the Lord because in God alone is his satisfaction and his strength. It is by that kind of deep trust that God's servants live (2 : 4).

When God Shines His Lamp

ZEPHANIAH must have preached at the same time as Jeremiah. The opening verse of his prophecy (1 : 1) fixes his ministry in the reign of King Josiah of Judah. Although Josiah was a good king and sought to be a dedicated and godly leader of his people, his famous reformation does not seem to have had a really lasting effect on the spiritual life of the southern kingdom. However, it may well be that the first section of Zephaniah's message to the people (1 : 2–9) reflects the low religious and moral condition of Judah prior to the Reformation and this prophet might have been used to influence the royal house and even have initiated some of the essential reforms. We know that the reforming movement was well under way (2 Chron. 34 : 1–7) before the discovery of the famous Book of the Law in the temple (2 Chron. 34 : 8–33).

The message contained in the *Book of Zephaniah* is addressed to six groups of people :

1. HYPOCRITICAL WORSHIPPERS
(Chapter 1, verses 1–8)

It is evident that the prophet was deeply distressed because of the dreadful insincerity of many of his fellow countrymen. Although outwardly they offered their elaborate sacrifices to God, in reality they secretly offered their adoration to heathen idols. He exposed the sin of 'those who bow down and swear to the Lord and yet swear by Milcom' (1 : 5). He knew that there were many throughout the land who had turned back from 'following the Lord, who do not seek the Lord or inquire of Him'.

2. DISHONEST MERCHANTS (Chapter 1, verses 9–18)

Zephaniah knew that Judah's low spiritual condition was reflected in her corrupt social, economic and commercial life. Many were 'leaping over the thresholds' (1 : 9) of conventional decency in order to plunder and rob their fellows. He warned the people who set up their stalls in the various market-places in Jerusalem that the Lord God would come upon them in judgment (1 : 10–11). Some imagined that God was not aware of their dishonesty but Zephaniah assured them that the Lord was active like a night-watchman searching Jerusalem with lamps. The light of His convicting presence would shine in their darkened minds to expose their wickedness. These evil traders suggested that God was not at all bothered about their business life as long as they offered their sacrifices: 'The Lord will not do good, nor will He do ill' (1 : 12). But Zephaniah said that these thieves would suffer the same fate as those they had robbed over the years (1 : 13) and in the moment of God's wrath their accumulated wealth would not be a scrap of use to them (1 : 18). Jeremiah said similar things in Jerusalem at about the same time (Jer. 15 : 13; 17 : 3; 20 : 5). Of what use is a bank balance if God is against a man?

3. HUMBLE SERVANTS (Chapter 2, verses 1–3)

Yet, for all this corruption, there were obviously some who put God first in their lives. Possibly others would join their ranks and seek God's forgiveness. While their greedy traders were seeking money, Zephaniah appealed to all serious minded people to seek the Lord (2 : 3) and so avert God's displeasure.

4. ARROGANT OPPRESSORS (Chapter 2, verses 4–15)

The prophet then proceeded to inveigh against the cruel sins of Judah's neighbours. Many of them were condemned for the way they had mocked God's people in their times of national distress (2 : 8, 10). Proud and arrogant oppressors, who boasted of their military supremacy and impregnable fortresses would all become desolate and forsaken.

5. DISCIPLINED CHILDREN (Chapter 3, verses 1–13)

Zephaniah cannot dwell for long on the sins of other countries without thinking again of disobedient and rebellious Jerusalem. What an indictment he issued against them. They were not attentive to God, they would not be corrected by God, they would not put their trust in God and they would not commune with God (3 : 2). Does this describe us? It is not set before us in Scripture merely as a shattering description of a seventh-century Hebrew city, but as a challenging warning to God's people in every generation. God's rebellious people would not listen to Him when He pleaded with them through the lips of many prophetic messengers (3 : 7, Jer. 2 : 29–30). Yet, because of the remnant of righteous people who did turn to Him, He would ultimately deliver them (3 : 11–13).

6. EXULTANT VICTORS (Chapter 3, verses 14–20)

Instead of being numbered among the persecuted millions, Judah would one day stand on its own feet.

God Himself would be in her midst as a mighty warrior (3:17). Once corrected and refined they would once again be established in a purified land to serve Him acceptably and bring Him great delight.

Give God First Place

THE last three 'minor prophets' of the Old Testament exercised their ministry in the post-exilic period, that is in the years after the Jewish people returned from their Babylonian captivity. In our chapters on *Ezra*, *Nehemiah* and *Isaiah* we have already commented on some aspects of this period of Hebrew history. In order to understand the message of *Haggai* we must look again at this less familiar period in the story of God's people and remind ourselves of some important background details. Once the captives were given permission to return to Judaea, expeditions were organised to lead the exiles home. In our study of *Ezra* we have traced some of the historical details of the return including the fact that once the foundation of the temple was laid the work on the temple site was interrupted and delayed by local opposition (Ezra 4 : 1–4 : 24). *Ezra* also makes it clear that the prophets who created the incentive to recommence this essential building programme were Haggai and Zechariah (Ezra 5 : 1). The *Book of Haggai* contains the substance of the prophet's message to the people at that time. From a reading of the book it becomes clear that severe drought over a considerable period of time had caused a succession of extremely poor harvests. This was spiritually and morally depressing as well as economically disastrous and it is against this kind of background that Haggai exercised his ministry. His teaching is contained in four distinct messages. Each address is given a precise date and covers one particular aspect of Haggai's prophetic word to the people of Judaea. The truths he sought to impress upon the people are still important and relevant to Christian people today. We might summarise them under the following headings:

1. ABOUT PRIORITIES (Chapter 1, verses 1–15)

Haggai's first word to the people was one of reproof. He told them that they had not put God first in their lives. They had given priority to materialistic issues. Many of them lived in splendid houses with luxuriously panelled walls while God's house had not been properly re-built (1 : 1–6). He points out that the poor crops were due to their spiritual disloyalty. The prophet must have been wonderfully encouraged by the eager response to his preaching. Within a few weeks, under the leadership of Zerubbabel, the governor, and Joshua, the high priest, a team of volunteers started work on the temple site.

2. ABOUT DESPONDENCY (Chapter 2, verses 1–9)

As the building programme continued it became obvious that the re-constructed temple was not going to be anything like as magnificent as the one built in the reign of Solomon and destroyed by the soldiers of Nebuchadnezzar. It is possible that some miserable onlookers had commented in a discouraging way on the difference between the two buildings but God's word through the prophet convinced them that the things which really mattered were assured. God's presence was clearly promised (2 : 4). Without that the temple would have been useless, no matter how splendid it might have looked. The building may not have looked as glorious as Solomon's but its value was to be reckoned by higher

M

standards altogether. God said quite clearly through His prophet that He would fill the house with His own splendour. Its glory would be in this—not in silver and gold (2:7). God also told His people that, having put Him first, He would give them prosperity (2:9) or 'peace' as the Authorised Version puts it. There was certainly no need for despondency. God had promised to be with them in abundant blessing.

3. ABOUT PURITY (Chapter 2, verses 10–19)

About two months after delivering his message of encouragement (2 : 1–9), Haggai was told to give a word of warning to God's people about impurity. It must be remembered that this very serious message was given in the context of the temple and its ritual. It emphasised the importance of being right with God *inwardly*. It is not enough to have a re-built temple if the lives of the worshippers were not clean before God. Haggai reminded the people that holy things used in God's service (vessels, garments, etc.) did not pass on their holiness to those who touched them, but anything regarded as unclean was certainly contagious (2:10–13). Their spiritual impurity was responsible for their economic poverty (2:14–17). God said that if their sins were confessed and put right then His blessing would follow (2:18–19).

4. ABOUT REWARD (Chapter 2, verses 20–23)

The four 'messages' preached by the prophet Haggai perfectly expound the words of the unnamed 'man of God' who, centuries before, told Eli the priest of God's promise 'those who honour Me, I will honour' (1 Sam. 2:30). The previous three messages were probably addressed to the whole company of returned exiles but

this final word was of a more personal nature. It concerned the welfare of the Judaean governor Zerubbabel
who, along with the high priest, had executed the
temple re-building programme. Zerubbabel was assured
of God's special favour. He had honoured God, so he
would be honoured. 'I will take you, O Zerubbabel my
servant . . . and make you like a signet ring, for I have
chosen you' (2 : 23). This man of God may have found
the work of leadership difficult and even costly, but the
Lord God assured him of present security and future
joys. He told Zerubbabel of a coming day when all who
oppose God's purposes will be finally overthrown (2 : 21–
22).

A View of the Beyond

No two of God's servants are exactly the same. One hymn assures us that 'there's a work for Jesus none but you can do'. It emphasises the profound biblical truth that God requires different types of people in order to further His work and accomplish His purposes. Haggai and Zechariah ministered to the same people at the same time (Ezra 5:1; 6:14; Hag. 2:1, 10; Zech. 1:1) and Zechariah appears to have been made aware of a call to preach between the second and third 'messages' of Haggai. Although these two men stood for similar ideals and had identical ambitions they were entirely different in personality, general outlook and approach but, in their different ways, God was pleased to use them both. Haggai was probably an older man and sympathetic with those who talked about the temple 'in its former glory' (2:3). Zechariah may have been a young man when he exercised his ministry (Zech. 2:4), but we cannot be certain. What is clear is that their method of communicating God's truth was vastly different although they were obviously aiming at the same results. In other words, although they had similar objectives they did not go about their tasks in exactly the same way. Haggai's message was delivered in down-to-earth, matter of fact prose. Zechariah appears to have been the youthful visionary. He endeavoured to communicate the same teaching as Haggai but did so by means of vivid pictures, simple visions with graphic and arresting portraiture which would impress themselves indelibly on the minds of those who listened to him.

Their difference in approach ought to be an immense encouragement to us all. God still uses different types of people to preach His Word and He can take hold of entirely dissimilar personalities and use them to the blessing of different people who need a particular kind of approach. The apostle Paul told the Corinthians that churches should not tolerate divisive and conflicting elements but form a harmonious whole and that members should work together as limbs in a human body (1. Cor. 12 : 4–31). It is pointless to complain that we do not have the same function and opportunity as someone else. We must work happily together and this will mean that we can serve effectively together. Haggai and Zechariah served side by side in a difficult enterprise and God was pleased to use these different types of men in His work.

The *Book of Zechariah* contains the prophet's teaching and can be divided into three parts.

1. THE HOLINESS OF GOD'S PEOPLE (Chapters 1–6)

The Book opens with a series of eight visions which were revealed to the prophet. The first (1 : 7–17) was of *four angelic riders* who had patrolled the earth and observed the sad condition of Jerusalem (1 : 12). This was obviously before the rebuilding of the temple (1 : 16) and the Lord assured His people that when His will was done and His Name honoured the city would once again be prosperous. The next vision was of *four horns*. Israel's enemies would be vanquished (1 : 18–21). The vision of the *measuring line* followed (2 : 1–13). The man who was taking the measurements of the city walls was told that it was not necessary for him to do this for God Himself would be her protecting wall (2 : 5). After this there was a vision of the *high priest* dressed in dirty robes—an unthinkable picture (3 : 1–10). It was not that the priest was himself sinful; he was a representative man and he carried the sins of God's people. They had to be cleansed (3 : 4–5). The next vision was of the *golden candlestick* (4 : 1–14). God's people were to be the bearers of light to others and all this was to be done in the power of God's Spirit (4 : 6). A vision followed of a *flying scroll* (5 : 1–4) —the word of God's judgment was made known to all. The seventh vision was of an *ephah* (5 : 5–11), a seven-gallon measure. Its message was unmistakably clear— all evil must be removed from the land. The prophet then saw a vision of *four chariots*, which came from between mountains of brass (6 : 1–8). It depicted God's sovereign rule and control over the whole earth. The prophet was asserting that world affairs were not determined by the kings of the Persian empire but by God Himself. There is an *epilogue* to this section which is of the ceremonial crowning of Joshua, the high priest. He was being honoured in this way as a means of foreshadowing the exaltation of the promised Messiah, the Priest-King, our Saviour Jesus Christ (6 : 9–15).

The main teaching of this section is an exposition of God's sovereignty and holiness. He rules over all the world and expects man's submission and purity. Sin must be cleansed and removed (3 : 3 f, 5 : 8–11) from our lives if we are to be used as His lights in this world (4 : 2–3, cf. Matt. 5 : 14–16; Phil. 2 : 15).

2. THE WORSHIP OF GOD'S PEOPLE (Chapters 7–8)

Two years later a deputation from Bethel asks whether certain fasts have to be observed. Zechariah's reply focuses attention on a familiar prophetic theme:

deeds of compassion (covenant-love) are far more accept-able in God's sight than the punctilious observance of any kind of ritual (7 : 8–12). The prophet anticipated a day when the lovelessness and spiritual indifference of the people would be changed to joyous prosperity and true worship (8 : 1–23).

3. THE DESTINY OF GOD'S PEOPLE (Chapters 9–14)

Like *Daniel*, the *Book of Zechariah* contains a type of literature we describe as 'apocalyptic'. Truths are com-municated by means of highly symbolic language and it is not always easy to discern the precise meaning of some of the ideas. The general meaning is plain enough, but those who wish to dogmatise regarding a particular interpretation of these chapters must always remember that equally sincere and devout Bible students have sometimes come to different conclusions!

In this final section the coming of the Messiah is vividly portrayed with a clear prediction of Israel's ultimate prosperity. This promised restoration would be delayed, however, by the people's rejection of their Messiah as a consequence of which the nation would enter upon some bitter conflicts and tribulations with other nations. After this the true people of God would acknowledge and worship Him as King (14 : 9, 16), and every thing in the Holy City and beyond would be given over entirely to God. 'Holiness to the Lord' would ul-timately be engraved on the nation's social, domestic and economic, as well as religious, life (14 : 20–21).

Over the centuries Christians have read this prophecy with both wonder and gratitude, recognising in its strik-ing portraiture none other than the Lord Jesus Christ, the Son of God, who came to this world as the triumphant yet lowly King, riding upon an ass, (9 : 9,

Matt. 21:4–5). Like the early Christian believers they have known Him to be the One who was pierced for us on the Cross (12:10, John 19:37) and they have worshipped Him as the Shepherd who was cruelly smitten (13:7, Matt. 26:31) that we might be saved (1 Pet. 2:24–25).

Love Offers its Best

THE last book of the Old Testament has both a backward and a forward look. The name *Malachi* means 'My messenger' and it may well be a pen-name given to a man who had some unpalatable truths to share with an extremely rebellious people. No date is given to the message but it obviously suits the period after the re-building of the temple for the sacrificial system had been maintained for some time. Some Old Testament scholars are persuaded that the message of the book best fits the period associated with the leadership and reforms of Nehemiah, but it is unwise to dogmatise on this question of date as there is no firm biblical evidence to guide us. About the message of *Malachi* nobody could possibly be in doubt. The book can be divided into two main sections in which the prophet told God's people of:

1. THEIR POVERTY (Chapters 1–2)

The prophet began by asserting the electing-love of God. Because He wanted to use His people God chose them and set His love upon them (1:2) but these children did not love Him in return. The priests had become bored with worship and offered poor sacrifices; any blind, sick or lame animals would do (1:6–13). What a way to treat a bountiful King (1:14)! The prophet addressed these corrupt priests with a word of severe warning (2:1–3) and reminded them of what God had

intended the priest to be—a man of reverent love
(2:4–5), helpful speech and blameless character (2:6).
Ideally he was to be used to turn people *from* iniquity
(2:6) but the priests of Malachi's day were, by their
spiritual and moral decadence, leading people *into*
iniquity (2:8–9). Malachi reiterated the important
prophetic theme that God did not accept sacrifices from
those whose lives were impure. Worship without love
was empty, meaningless ritualism, and it offended God
(2:10–17).

2. THEIR PROSPECTS (Chapters 3–4)

God uses the prophet to tell these loveless worshippers
that a Messenger was to come with a purifying ministry.
He would be so effectively used that men would ultimately offer acceptable offerings to God (3:1–5). The
people of God were urged to present their best to God
(3:6–12) and not to speak hastily and casually about
spiritual things (3:7–15). Those who worshipped Him
in sincerity did not say damaging things but helpful
things to each other and God knew this (3:16–18). A
day of judgment awaited those who were arrogant and
impenitent, but a new and glorious day was in store for
those who truly adored Him (4:1–3).

The Book ends with both a backward and a forward
look. It reminds God's people of the importance of
entire obedience—'Remember the law of my servant
Moses' (4:4). It also closes on the note of compassionate appeal—a prophet would arise, like Elijah, who
would call the people back to God's Word and beg them
to repent (4:4–6). A few hundred years later this promised prophetic figure, John the Baptist, appeared in
the wilderness regions of Judaea. As the divinely
appointed herald he was used to bring many people of

all types to a genuine repentance (Matt. 3 : 1–10; 11 : 7–
15). Perhaps his greatest moment was when he publicly
identified the Lord Jesus Christ as the Lamb of God who
would bear away the sin of the world (John 1 : 29). John
was a forerunner, content to be an appealing voice
(John 1 : 6–8; 3 : 27–28). Like Malachi, his prophetic
predecessor, it was enough to be known by God as 'My
messenger'.

Our study of the Old Testament has come to an end,
but the names of Moses and Elijah in its closing book
are surely meant to impress two great Old Testament
truths upon our minds : Moses says 'Obey God' (Malachi
4.4) and Elijah says 'Tell others' (Mal. 4 : 5–6). If
biblical truths are to be of the greatest spiritual value
they must be both appropriated and shared.

Old Testament Kings and Prophets
(Approximate dates of accession shown in brackets)

THE UNITED KINGDOM
SAUL (1045)
DAVID (1010)
SOLOMON (970)

THE DIVIDED KINGDOM

JUDAH (Southern Kingdom)		PROPHETS To Judah To Israel		ISRAEL (Northern Kingdom)		OTHER NATIONS
Rehoboam	(931)			Jeroboam I	(931)	
Abijah	(913)					
Asa	(911)			Nadab	(910)	Probable period of
				Baasha	(909)	writing of Homers
				Elah	(886)	epics (900)
				Zimri	(885)	
				Tibni	(885)	
				Omri	(885)	
Jehoshaphat	(873)		Elijah	Ahab	(874)	
Jehoram	(853)			Ahaziah	(853)	
			Elisha	Jehoram	(852)	Foundation of
Ahaziah	(841)			Jehu	(841)	Carthage (850)
Athaliah (Queen)	(841)					
Joash	(835)	?JOEL				
Amaziah	(796)			Jehoahaz	(814)	
				Jehoash	(798)	
				Jeroboam II	(793)	
Uzziah (Azariah)	(790)	ISAIAH	AMOS HOSEA JONAH			
				Zechariah	(753)	Foundation of Rome
				Shallum	(752)	(753)
Jotham	(751)	MICAH		*Menahem	(752)	Assyrian power at its greatest.
				Pekahiah	(741)	Accession of Tiglath Pileser III (745)
Ahaz	(735)			*Pekah	(752)	Assyrian invasion of
Hezekiah	(728)			Hoshea	(731)	Israel
Manasseh	(696)			FALL OF SAMARIA	(722)	
Amon	(642)					
Josiah	(639)	JEREMIAH ZEPHANIAH NAHUM HABAKKUK		* Menahem (752–742) and Pekah (752–732) were rival kings and probably occupied the throne at the same period		End of Assyrian power. Ninevah destroyed (612) Battle of Megiddo— Josiah against Egyptian armies.
Jehoahaz	(609)					Josiah killed (609)

JUDAH (Southern Kingdom)	PROPHETS To Judah To Israel	ISRAEL (Northern Kingdom)	OTHER NATIONS
Jehoiakim (608) Jehoiachin (597) (Jerusalem captured 597)	EZEKIEL (to Babylonian exiles)		Judah in hands of Egyptians for a few years, then under Babylonian domination. Period of Babylonian power (612–538) Egyptian armies defeated by Babylonians at Carchemish (605)
Zedekiah (597) (Jerusalem destroyed 586)			
	THE EXILE ? OBADIAH (to poor communities left in Judaea) THE RETURN *Prophets* (probable date of ministry in brackets)		
Leaders (probable date of return in brackets) Sheshbazzar } Zerubbabel } (538)	HAGGAI } ZECHARIAH } (520)		Babylon taken by Cyrus (538) Foundation of Roman Republic (509) Iron Age beginning in Britain (500) Socrates born (470) Death of Confucius (479)
Ezra (458) Nehemiah (445)	MALACHI (450)		

Index to Books of the Old Testament

Genesis 9
Exodus 15
Leviticus 22
Numbers 28
Deuteronomy 35
Joshua 42
Judges 49
Ruth 55
Samuel, 1 & 2 60
Kings, 1 & 2 70
Chronicles, 1 & 2 83
Ezra 91
Nehemiah 97
Esther 102
Job 105
Psalms 110
Proverbs 113
Ecclesiastes 117

Song of Solomon 120
Isaiah 124
Jeremiah 130
Lamentations 134
Ezekiel 135
Daniel 139
Hosea 143
Joel 148
Amos 151
Obadiah 156
Jonah 158
Micah 161
Nahum 166
Habakkuk 169
Zephaniah 172
Haggai 176
Zechariah 180
Malachi 185